DATE DUE

DEMCO 38-296

GREAT WRITERS OF THE ENGLISH LANGUAGE

Adventure Writers

STAFF CREDITS

Executive Editor
Reg Wright

Series Editor
Sue Lyon

Editors
Jude Welton
Sylvia Goulding

Deputy Editors
Alice Peebles
Theresa Donaghey

Features Editors
Geraldine McCaughrean
Emma Foa
Ian Chilvers

Art Editors
Kate Sprawson
Jonathan Alden
Helen James

Designers
Simon Wilder
Frank Landamore

Senior Picture Researchers
Julia Hanson
Vanessa Fletcher
Georgina Barker

Picture Clerk
Vanessa Cawley

Production Controllers
Judy Binning
Tom Helsby

Editorial Secretaries
Fiona Bowser
Sylvia Osborne

Managing Editor
Alan Ross

Editorial Consultant
Maggi McCormick

Publishing Manager
Robert Paulley

Reference Edition Published 1989
Published by Marshall Cavendish Corporation
147 West Merrick Road
Freeport, Long Island
N.Y. 11520

Typeset by Litho Link Ltd., Welshpool
Printed and Bound in Italy by
L.E.G.O. S.p.a. Vicenza

LIBRARY OF CONGRESS
Library of Congress Cataloging-in-Publication Data
Great Writers of the English Language
    p. cm.
    Includes index vol.
    ISBN 1-85435-000-5 (set): $399.95
    1. English literature — History and criticism. 2. English
literature — Stories, plots, etc. 3. American literature — History
and criticism. 4. American literature — Stories, plots, etc.
5. Authors. English — Biography. 6. Authors. American — Biography.
I. Marshall Cavendish Corporation.
PR85.G66 1989
820'.9 – dc19   88-21077
                                                          CIP

ISBN 1–85435–000–5 (set)
ISBN 1–85435–011–0 (vol)

GREAT WRITERS OF THE ENGLISH LANGUAGE

Adventure Writers

Daniel Defoe

Sir Walter Scott

Robert Louis Stevenson

Rudyard Kipling

MARSHALL CAVENDISH · NEW YORK · TORONTO · LONDON · SYDNEY

CONTENTS

DANIEL DEFOE

←◆ *c.1660-1731* ◆→

No easy judgement can be passed on this pioneer of the novel
and of journalism, whose greatest success was the world classic
Robinson Crusoe. Daniel Defoe was alternately devious and
straightforward, secretive and open. His passionate belief in
freedom of conscience was equalled by his enthusiasm for
colonial expansion and mercantile enterprise. His writing
reflects his own opinion that 'whatever concerns mankind is
of interest to me'.

Merchant Venturer

A 17th-century entrepreneur – albeit a resoundingly unsuccessful one – Daniel Defoe tried his hand at all manner of business before turning government spy and propagandist.

Robinson Crusoe and Daniel Defoe are inseparable. Yet the fictional castaway seems more real than either his creator or the real-life character he drew on for his best-known book. This paradox would have intrigued Defoe as much as later accolades given to his massive literary output. For although his achievements as a novelist rank as immortal, they were in a sense incidental to his life-long activities as merchant venturer, traveller, historian, Government agent and pamphleteer.

Daniel Foe was born in the City of London during the latter half of 1660 or early 1661. Due to imperfectly kept parish registers, the exact date is unknown. He was the youngest of three children. His sisters Mary and Elizabeth were born in 1657 and 1659 respectively.

The Foe household lived in close harmony. Daniel's father, James Foe, was an honest, hard-working butcher and candle-maker of Flemish descent, whose immediate ancestors had been yeomen or small farmers in Northamptonshire. They anglicized the original Defawe(?), which Daniel revived in modified form but without an official name change, probably during his twenties or thirties – partly as affectation, perhaps also for the reason he jested about: the inconvenience of the name Foe for someone so often engaged in public controversy.

Sadly, the facts about Daniel's mother are scarce and vague. Her name was Alice, and she may have been the daughter of a Somerset squire. No known record exists of her marriage or death. It is thought she died between 1665 and 1671. That she was a sensible woman is evident from this anecdote among Daniel's recollections of his childhood: "If you vex me, I'll eat no dinner, said I . . . till my mother taught me to be wiser, by letting

Daniel Defoe
Much about Defoe remains a mystery – his precise date of birth, his mother's ancestry, whole chapters of his life. He was obsessed with anonymity, spent much of his time on the run and was destined to die alone.

Thames vistas
As a child, Daniel could watch the "draught and reflux of the mighty river" from his window, his imagination fired by thoughts of what lay beyond.

me stay till I was hungry." This was his only written reference to her, though his writings perpetually show respect, even reverence, for a woman's part in the family.

Although not rich, James Foe was prosperous enough to afford his only son an exceptional education – initially at Reverend James Fisher's 12-room school near Box Hill, Darking (modern Dorking), Surrey, and subsequently at Reverend Charles Morton's Academy in Newington Green (then a village just north of London). Both teachers were Independent ministers. Morton, later vice-president of Harvard College, was a brilliant tutor who opened boys' minds to the wonders of the world and, Defoe recalled, filled them with "all parts of academic learning", unusu-

ally for the time, including science in the school curriculum.

Indeed, the tuition there was broader than at Oxford or Cambridge, from which Daniel was barred as the son of a religious Nonconformist, or Dissenter. Morton's clarity of expression and natural writing style served as models for Daniel, who was already a voracious reader; so, too, did John Bunyan and the Bible.

A small and sickly youth – his adult height was about 5ft 6in – with sharp features, grey eyes and dark-brown hair, Daniel was nonetheless a 'toughie' who relished most sports, notably boxing, wrestling and swimming. As a young man, he carried a 'flail' (blackjack), more for swagger than to use against those impertinent enough to taunt him

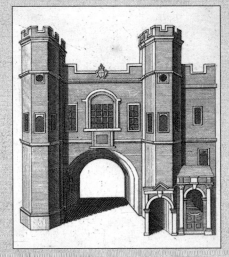

Mansell Collection

Mansell Collection

Roots and heritage
Daniel was born in the parish of St Giles, Cripplegate (far left), which lay just beyond the northern outskirts of the City. His father, James Foe, was a butcher and chandler by trade, and had a butcher's shop on Fore Street, near Moorgate. By virtue of this, Daniel applied for membership of and was admitted into the Butchers' Company (guild) years later.

Key Dates

c.1660 born in London

c.1683 sets up as wholesale merchant

1684 marries Mary Tuffley

1685 joins Monmouth's Rebellion

c.1687 publishes a pamphlet, attacking James II

1688 becomes friend and agent of William III

1692 bankrupt for £17,000

1702 *The Shortest Way with the Dissenters*

1703 in Newgate Prison; pilloried for seditious libel

1704 starts the *Review* journal; engaged as Government agent

1719 *Robinson Crusoe*

1722 *Moll Flanders; A Journal of the Plague Year*

1731 dies in London

A-on: Westminster Bridge/Private Collection/Bridgeman Art Library

about the large mole near his mouth. He rarely feared physical violence.

Daniel was intended for ministry in the dissenting Presbyterian Church. But in autumn 1681 he realized he felt no vocation. If his father was disappointed, he never blamed Daniel, who remained a firm friend to Dissenters and represented them at all levels. Nationalist in outlook, he always maintained diversity of faith should not mean disunity of purpose or effort.

CITY BUSINESS

Instead of pursuing a religious career, Defoe went into business, becoming "a convert to the principles of merchandising", as Crusoe said of himself. Through informal instruction in management, probably from his father's acquaintances, he soon grew proficient and by the age of 23 was successfully established with a warehouse and living quarters at Freeman's Yard, Cornhill, close to the Royal Exchange.

Beginning modestly with haberdashery, Defoe soon graduated to the widest range of commodities — everything from cheese, wine and seafood to tobacco, timber and wool – anything on which a profit could be made by shrewd wholesale buying and selling. These were stirring times, with trade booming and new markets emerging. Defoe did substantial business with Spain, Portugal and the American colonies, direct or through agents.

On one voyage to Rotterdam, he was snatched by roving Algerian pirates but quickly released, through rescue by another ship or payment of a ransom. He was as vague on this point as about a probable smuggling trip to France he undertook with other merchants.

In a life dogged by as much misfortune as good luck, there were certain risks where Defoe judged

National Portrait Gallery, London

Festivities on ice
On 1 January 1684, Defoe married the young Mary Tuffley, during the coldest spell of weather in living memory. The River Thames had frozen over so solidly that a week-long fair could be held on the ice (above), complete with roasted oxen and the sport of bear baiting.

Monmouth's Rebellion
A year after his wedding, Defoe joined the ill-fated attempt by Charles II's illegitimate son, the Duke of Monmouth (left), to claim the English crown. He challenged the despotic Catholic King James II at the Battle of Sedgemoor. Monmouth, with hundreds of his supporters, was caught and executed.

silence the better part of valour; had he revealed the hazards, those who funded his deals could have been dissuaded from further lending. Mystery shrouds these financiers' identities. They may have included wealthy Dissenters. About one source of money, however, there is no shadow of doubt – the £3700 dowry brought by his wife, Mary Tuffley, the only daughter of a well-to-do City maker of wine casks.

Mary was bright, lively, fashion-conscious and aged about 20 when she went to the altar of St Botolph, Aldgate, with the well-dressed young merchant on the morning of 1 January 1684. Their wedding was elaborate, although no honeymoon followed. They simply took a romantic ride in a hackney coach through snowbound streets to Freeman's Yard, the first of their many homes in London.

They remained married for 47 years and retained deep affection for each other. Of their eight children, six survived into adulthood. Mary was a devoted wife and good manager who would not "diminish one penny" any money entrusted to her, Defoe declared – who later admitted he had "ruined" her fortunes.

Their relationship was strained by Defoe's frequent absences on various ventures. The most dangerous of these was his part in Monmouth's Rebellion of June 1685. In a flush of enthusiasm

A. Hondius: Frost Fair on the Thames. The Museum of London

William III

Enthusiastic about the Dutch Prince, William of Orange, Defoe rode out to welcome him at the start of the Glorious Revolution in November 1688. He continued to admire and support the monarch throughout his 13-year reign, hailing him as "the glorious, Great, and Good and Kind", and became his leading pamphleteer. William was prepared to go to war with France in order to curtail her power and protect English trade. Defoe argued strongly for this view in two political pamphlets, and also addressed the question on religious grounds. In The Danger of the Protestant Religion Consider'd, *he sought to alert his fellow countrymen to the papist 'threat' from across the Channel.*

National Portrait Gallery, London

for the Duke's crusade against the despotic Catholic King, James II, Defoe saddled his horse, secretly left London, and joined the insurgents just before the Battle of Sedgemoor, where he was among those routed in the first encounter. Three of his former classmates who also took part were caught and executed along with hundreds more rebels and the Duke of Monmouth himself. Defoe managed to escape and may briefly have taken refuge on the Continent.

It was there that he issued one of his first political pamphlets – an attack on King James, who fled into exile and was succeeded in the Glorious Revolution of 1688 by the Dutch prince who had long plotted to topple him: William of Orange. Defoe was among those who rode out to welcome the clever but cold-hearted new monarch.

Despite their difference in rank, the two men had much in common. Both were self-righteous zealots ahead of their time. Both believed in a united kingdom. And above all, both were outsiders through circumstance and character – a foreign prince, and a merchant whose Puritan idealism outweighed his business sense, and was partly expressed through his talent as a writer. Defoe remained a friend and loyal supporter of the sovereign he called *"William, the Glorious, Great, and Good, and Kind"* and became his leading pamphleteer.

Fact or Fiction

Mansell Collection

THE ORIGINAL CASTAWAY

The real-life Robinson Crusoe was not a disciplined, God-fearing character, but the rough, dour Scotsman, Alexander Selkirk. Born in 1676, he went to sea aged 19 and joined a band of pirates in the Pacific. It was there that Selkirk was put ashore in 1704 – at his own request – after arguing with his shipmates, on an uninhabited island 400 miles west of Chile.

Somehow Selkirk survived, although he had virtually lost the power of speech when he was rescued over four years later.

Back in Britain, his adventures made headline news and Defoe drew heavily on contemporary accounts in creating his hero.

Mary Evans Picture Library

Defoe felt it impossible not to be involved in politics. Yet even had he stuck to business, he probably would have gone bankrupt in 1692. His failure was partly attributable to the losses he sustained through insuring ships that were seized or destroyed in the war with France. The underlying reason, however, was lack of judgement in over-committing himself; he had inherited all his father's acumen, none of his caution.

DEBTORS' PRISON

In total, Defoe's debts amounted to a crushing £17,000. Marine war risks were then a personal matter and not, as now, a national obligation. Worse, debtors could still be imprisoned to prevent abuse of credit. In one of his tracts, Defoe complained bitterly that England was the only country which punished debtors by rendering them incapable of paying off their debts. He himself was confined in the infamous Newgate Prison for more than a week but, ever a persuasive talker, reached honourable agreement to repay his 140 or so creditors 15s in the £.

Within 10 years, he had discharged all but £5000 of his debts, and re-entered 'the vast ocean of trade' as a brick and pantile manufacturer at Tilbury, Essex. The new venture also failed, and Defoe was never again free of debt. Some creditors, perhaps enraged at his love of good living, hounded him savagely. In Bristol, where he once fled to dodge them, he was known as 'The Sunday

"An Emblem of Hell"
Thousands of pounds in debt, Defoe was committed to Newgate Prison (above) in 1692 to await trial. Years later, he described his sensation on seeing it through his heroine Moll Flanders: "I was carried to Newgate . . . My very blood chills at the mention of its Name . . . the hellish Noise, the Roaring, Swearing and Clamour, the Stench and Nastiness . . . joyn'd to make the Place seem an Emblem of Hell itself."

WHIGS AND TORIES

Whigs were progressive upholders of popular rights; Tories, instead, believed in the divine right of kings and represented landed interests. Defoe hoped vainly to see them reconciled.

A Whig & Tory, a Wrestling
Angry and Fierce are both, both very Bold,
Long did they struggle, yet maintain'd their Hold.
Both did stand out against the Kick and Trip,
But the poor Whig is got upon the Hip:
And after all his pains & sweat and toil,
Is like to get a Fall, at least a Foil.
And now the Tory has him, tis well known,
And has with strength & Judgment Cast him down.

Fotomas

gentleman' – Sunday being the only day he could walk about free from the threat of arrest.

The law overpowered him again – this time for alleged seditious libel as author of *The Shortest Way with the Dissenters* (1702), an ironic attack against the tyranny of "high-fliers" – High Church Tories. It achieved wide sales, but was completely misunderstood. Defoe managed to elude the State prosecution for months through hair's breadth escapes – more than once by jumping from windows as the authorities pounced. The persistence of the law enforcers was arguably a bid by the ruling Tories to compel the writer into revealing information that would discredit the Whig opposition and the reign of William III, who died in 1702.

The Shortest Way was publicly burnt by the common hangman. On his lawyer's advice, Defoe pleaded guilty and threw himself on the London Assize Court's mercy, despite having satirized one of the judges as brutal and corrupt. Their sentence was predictably harsh: a £200 fine, three appearances in the pillory, and seven years' "good behaviour" (i.e. silence in print).

The pillorying was postponed three weeks by appeals, and Defoe's apprehension grew; for someone who craved anonymity, the fear of public ridicule was worse than the threat of maiming or death from objects hurled by the mob. Tory pamphleteers were already taunting him as "the prophet Dan" in the "lions' den" of Newgate. During his time in prison, Defoe wrote his *Hymn to the Pillory*.

POPULAR HERO

Queen Anne did "not think fit to delay any longer". Towards noon on Thursday, 29 July 1703, Defoe mounted a platform outside the Royal Exchange and allowed his neck and wrists to be clamped in the "wooden ruff" crosspiece of the crucifix-like pillory. An extraordinary thing then happened. Instead of being pelted with filth, he was cheered; justly recognizing his courage, the crowd applauded his defence of their liberties. The *Hymn* had turned his punishment into triumph.

The outraged authorities left him in Newgate for a further three months. Then, in a reversal typical of that era's labyrinthine politics, he was freed and pardoned. The Queen paid his fine, and Defoe was appointed at £200 a year to promote the Government's interests through his writings. The *Review*, one of 26 journals he was involved with, became his weekly platform.

Defoe wrote Government propaganda during the rest of his life, for whichever party was in power, and this led to accusations of "turncoat". He also embarked on active service as a secret agent (under the codename of "Alexander Goldsmith"), notably helping bring about the

J. Crowther: St Giles Cripplegate/Guildhall Library/Bridgeman Art Library

Parish of St Giles
Defoe was born, lived and died in the Parish of St Giles, Cripplegate (above), dying just a few yards from the spot where he was thought to have been born. He was buried in Bunhill Fields Cemetery.

1707 Act of Union with Scotland. He also infiltrated and "toned down" anti-Government publications – to save hot-headed writers from persecution, he claimed. His political ideal was moderate government for maximum public benefit. Though prosecuted again, he never abandoned his independent stance, whether writing on religion and current affairs or economics, manners and morals.

He learned shorthand and wasted nothing seen or heard. All re-emerged in masterly works like his *Tour Through the Whole Island of Great Britain* and the haunting *Journal of the Plague Year* that heralded the best modern journalism. "Illiterate" – a jibe that hurt him more than any other – and "a truly great liar" were slurs cast in an age when the greater the truth, the greater the criticism. Defoe took conspicuous care *not* to accept rumour but to gain facts, as essential for rational opinion.

The greatest literary triumph of the 'lonely Man of Letters' was *Robinson Crusoe*, a 'faction' tale so skilfully blending realism and romance that after publication on 25 April 1719, it was widely believed to be a true story.

Crusoe earned "deliverance from evil". Defoe earned little from the book or his other renowned and sympathetic studies of solitaries, *Moll Flanders* and *Colonel Jack*. He died, probably alone, of "a lethargy" – exhaustion – at a lodging house in Ropemaker's Alley, close to his presumed birthplace, on 24 April 1731. Few witnessed his burial in Bunhill Fields.

Tillemans: Queen Anne in the House of Lords (detail). Reproduced by gracious permission of Her Majesty the Queen.

Royal powers
Queen Anne (above) was intent on controlling political writing and in Parliament argued for laws to be passed to that effect. She condoned Defoe's imprisonment and subsequent pillorying (right) for seditious libel, and yet, when public opinion turned, it was she who freed him and paid his fine.

ROBINSON CRUSOE

One of fiction's great survivors, Robinson Crusoe, through sheer perseverance, turns a menacing wilderness into an imitation of old England – with all its good and ills.

Brazilian prologue
After suffering one shipwreck and being enslaved by the Turks, Crusoe arrives in Brazil (right), where he observes the planters "and how they grew rich suddenly". But after two or three years' effort, he is restless and sees his life as staid: "I could have done this as well in England, among my friends, as have gone five thousand miles off to do it among strangers and savages." The wanderlust has once again gripped him and he cannot resist.

Few themes have exerted such a grip on the imagination of writers and readers alike as that of an individual stranded on a desert island, and no-one has explored it with greater power and imagination than Daniel Defoe in *Robinson Crusoe*. Like Crusoe, Defoe was a pioneer: *Robinson Crusoe* is an early landmark of fiction, one of the first great novels to create a realistic imaginative world, to tell a fascinating story, to point a moral and to invest an ordinary character with the stature of myth. Its novelty was the combination of a fictional tale with the impression of autobiographical authenticity.

GUIDE TO THE PLOT
The story is told exclusively from Crusoe's point of view. At the outset, he presents himself as an impetuous young man intent on confronting and challenging his destiny. Disregarding his father's advocacy of the "middle station of life", where a young man might advance steadily through application and industry, he decides to seek adventure and his fortune through life at sea instead.

Storms and general ill luck seem to dog his career (a comrade interprets this as a bad omen), and on one voyage his ship is attacked by pirates. Crusoe is sent into slavery in Sallee, a port belonging to the Moors. With the aid of the youth Xury – whom he later sells as a slave – he manages to escape, and is picked up by a Portuguese ship whose captain takes him to Brazil. There Crusoe becomes a planter.

Yet when the opportunity arises years later, he cannot resist the temptation to go on another voyage and thus avoid an involuntary slide into the "middle station of life". This time he sets out to the Guinea coast, where – he convinces the other planters – it was easy "to purchase upon the coast, for trifles – such as beads, toys, knives, scissors, hatchets, bits of glass, and the like – not only gold-dust, Guinea grains, elephants' teeth, etc., but negroes, for the service of the Brazils, in great numbers". Although Crusoe suspects he is tempting Providence, he cannot resist: "But I, that was born to be my own destroyer, could no more resist the offer than I could restrain my first rambling designs when my father's good counsel was lost upon me."

His misgivings are justified, for the ship is wrecked, the crew drowns, and Robinson Crusoe alone is cast ashore on an uninhabited island. At first distraught at his situation, he comes to acknowledge his luck at being alive and also his good fortune that the ship has been washed up on a rock accessible by raft. He makes repeated journeys to the wreck and collects provisions and every bit of material that might come in useful.

He then spends some years building a permanent shelter as well as a "country-house", hunting for food, exploring the island, and trying to recreate the standard of living he is accustomed to. He produces tools, grows barley and rice, and domesticates goats and parrots.

His achievement is to create things he would normally take for granted – such as his daily bread, or clothes – without proper tools or knowledge of their production: "I must not omit to acknowledge that they were wretchedly made; for if I was a bad carpenter, I was a worse tailor."

Mansell Collection

A father's advice
Having lost two sons already, Robinson's father begs him to stay home and pursue "the middle station" rather than adventure.

"*I travelled for discovery up to the top of that hill, where after I had . . . got to the top, I saw my fate to my great affliction – viz., that I was in an island environed in every way with the sea: no land to be seen.*"

He even tries to build a boat, then realizes it is too heavy to be moved to the sea.

As Crusoe recounts his practical response to his plight, he also gives an insight into his spiritual progress. His moods understandably veer between desperation at his isolation and gratitude at his salvation. Prompted by fear in the face of earthquakes and illness, he starts to read the Bible which he has salvaged from the wreckage, and develops a religious understanding and an awareness of his previous "dreadful life, perfectly destitute of the knowledge and fear of God".

He reflects that "we never see the true state of our condition till it is illustrated to us by its contraries", and begins to feel "how much more happy this life I now led was, with all its miserable circumstances, than the wicked, cursed abominable life I led all the past part of my days". By his eleventh year on the island, he has come to see the good fortune of being stranded here: "What a table was here spread for me in a wilderness, where I saw nothing at first but to perish for hunger!"

However, in one of the great moments of fiction, his complacency is shattered

Shipwrecked!

"We all saw plainly, that the sea went so high that the boat could not escape and that we should be inevitably drowned." But by the sheerest luck, a wave carries Crusoe ashore when all his shipmates are lost. The wreck lingers where it has run aground, and while it holds intact, Crusoe pillages it for every manner of useful tool and material and means of survival (top right), using a raft to ferry his finds ashore.

Home from home

"Having settled my household staff and habitation", (right) "made me a table and chair, and all as handsome about me as I could, I began . . . to keep my journal; of which I shall here give you a copy."

The "hope that God would hear"
One critic has written of the religious elements in Robinson Crusoe, *that Crusoe's faith 'like everything else about him on the island . . . is homemade and not of the finest quality . . . it is sound and it will stand up to daily use' (left). He experiences a 'sense of God's goodness', strives to convert Friday, and attributes his deliverance entirely to the beneficence of God.*

"Exceedingly surprised"
After seven years' solitude, Crusoe finds the single "print of a man's naked foot on the shore" (right). It shatters his complacent self-reliance and fills him with terror: "never frightened hare fled to cover, or fox to earth, with more terror of mind than I." For three days he dares not leave his cave, and struggles with loss of faith as well as the more practical worries of how to ensure his survival.

when one morning he comes across a human footprint in the sand. It is a premonition of a time when the island will no longer be his alone. Later, when finding a gruesome array of skulls, bones and skeletons spread on the beach, he becomes aware of the danger from cannibals who visit the island, and for the next few years lives in exaggerated fear of meeting them. Yet it is some years before he does have an encounter with the cannibals, driving them away with musket and sword and, in the process, rescuing a man he names after the day on which they meet: Friday.

Man Friday becomes Crusoe's faithful companion for the next few years on the island, worshipping Crusoe as his saviour and father, learning to speak English, and eventually renouncing his heathen god, Benamuckee, to embrace his master's 'superior' Christianity. Yet Friday's appearance is an augury that the days of Crusoe's splendid isolation are numbered.

AN ECCENTRIC HERO
As with most classic novels, part of the greatness of *Robinson Crusoe* lies in its wide appeal and the diversity of themes it develops. As a children's book, it contains all the ingredients of the best adventure stories – pirates, shipwreck, mutineers, cannibals, and the plight of a castaway on an island with only animals for company. But it all seems true: Crusoe's mastery of his environment – his efforts to make a table or milk a goat or grow a patch of barley – is, for example, described in such detail as to seem real. It bears the stamp of popular contemporary travelogues.

The main fascination, however, is the complexity and eccentricity of Crusoe's

character: his frequent changes of mood and mind, jumping between reason and impulse; his utilitarian attitude to religion, where God is adopted as a sort of spiritual business partner; his colonial attitude to Xury and later Friday (despite the facts that Crusoe himself has experienced the indignity of slavery and has been longing for a friend and companion); and his unromantic attitude to his surroundings, where the wonders of nature are not admired so much as analysed, then categorized and catalogued according to their value to Man. The main theme is undoubtedly the character of Crusoe and his triumph as an individual.

On one level, Crusoe is an 18th-century

version of the Prodigal Son. In defiance of his father, he has embarked on a reckless life of adventure which, after various portents of doom, has culminated in shipwreck and isolation on the island. There he has learnt repentance, true Christianity, and renewed obedience to God the Father. The Prodigal Son theme is emphasized by Crusoe's frequent allusions to the biblical story: "Had I now had the sense to have gone back to Hull, and have gone home, I had been happy, and my father, an emblem of our blessed Saviour's parable, had even killed the fatted calf for me." The father-son theme is an insistent one in the novel, to the point where Friday's loyalty and affection

Poll the parrot
The phrases Crusoe trains his parrot (left) to say give a telling insight into his self-pity, for he teaches it to say, "Poor Robin Crusoe! Where are you? Where have you been?"

"A worse tailor"
When his clothes wear out, Crusoe makes more out of cured skins, and a "great clumsy goat-skin umbrella . . . the most necessary thing I had about me, next to my gun" (above right).

"His name should be Friday"
Crusoe describes the native he rescues from cannibals as "a comely, handsome fellow" of about 26, "European in his countenance", and therefore (by implication) a tolerable companion. Crusoe "taught him to say master, and then let him know that was to be my name."

towards Crusoe are defined as being "like those of a child to a father".

On a philosophical level, Crusoe stands for Man himself *as an island*, a state of isolation he must and does bear with courage and fortitude. Crusoe's behaviour is an affirmation of human strength and endurance, and the capacity of Man to overcome physical and psychological adversity. The appearance of Friday is then a sort of seal of approval, a perspective against which Crusoe's achievement can be measured. As Friday's instant respect and reverence show, Crusoe's semi-civilized life on the island has not diminished his dignity and authority.

Crusoe is also a model of 18th-century Man, not only a product of, but an advertisement for, the Age of Reason. By applying rational thought to every situation and by reproducing the skills learnt from civilization, he tames his environment and saves himself from degenerating into savagery. His relative absence of imagination and his blindness to the awesomeness of Nature become positive virtues, for they do not interfere with his strictly logical solutions to the problem of survival.

There is a telling incident when Crusoe discovers some gold coins on the wreck

"*To think that it was all my own; that I was king and lord of all this country indefeasibly, and had a right of possession . . .*"

In the Background

THE SLAVE TRADE

Crusoe is both a slave and a slave owner at a time when the slave trade thrived uncriticized. The New World plantations created an enormous demand for labour, and the Black Triangle emerged. Ships sailed from Europe to Africa to trade goods for slaves. The slaves were shipped to the New World – although many died on the way – and sold for money, sugar or cotton brought back to Europe.

SECTION OF VESSEL, SHOWING THE MANNER OF STOWING SLAVES ON BOARD.

and loftily dismisses them as useless for his present difficulties: "'O drug!' said I aloud, 'what art thou good for? Thou art not worth to me . . .'"; but then, "upon second thoughts", he takes them anyway. Defoe no doubt felt he was only representing how someone in that situation might credibly behave, but the scene speaks volumes about Crusoe's mercantile ideas and the materialist society that he lived in. In the Romantic era, Crusoe would often be viewed as a soulless man who never even admired a sunset; but today he is judged by his self-reliance and determination. *Robinson Crusoe* presents a new face to each succeeding age – one reason that both novel and hero survive so well.

15

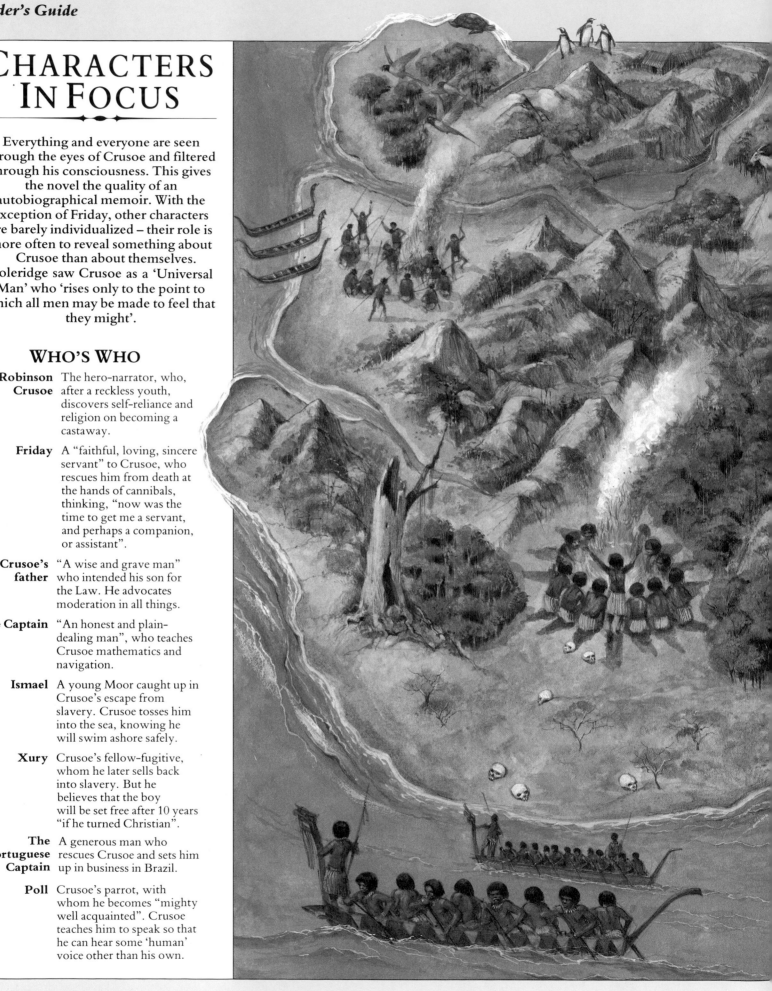

CHARACTERS IN FOCUS

Everything and everyone are seen through the eyes of Crusoe and filtered through his consciousness. This gives the novel the quality of an autobiographical memoir. With the exception of Friday, other characters are barely individualized – their role is more often to reveal something about Crusoe than about themselves. Coleridge saw Crusoe as a 'Universal Man' who 'rises only to the point to which all men may be made to feel that they might'.

WHO'S WHO

Robinson Crusoe The hero-narrator, who, after a reckless youth, discovers self-reliance and religion on becoming a castaway.

Friday A "faithful, loving, sincere servant" to Crusoe, who rescues him from death at the hands of cannibals, thinking, "now was the time to get me a servant, and perhaps a companion, or assistant".

Crusoe's father "A wise and grave man" who intended his son for the Law. He advocates moderation in all things.

The Captain "An honest and plain-dealing man", who teaches Crusoe mathematics and navigation.

Ismael A young Moor caught up in Crusoe's escape from slavery. Crusoe tosses him into the sea, knowing he will swim ashore safely.

Xury Crusoe's fellow-fugitive, whom he later sells back into slavery. But he believes that the boy will be set free after 10 years "if he turned Christian".

The Portuguese Captain A generous man who rescues Crusoe and sets him up in business in Brazil.

Poll Crusoe's parrot, with whom he becomes "mighty well acquainted". Crusoe teaches him to speak so that he can hear some 'human' voice other than his own.

Robinson Crusoe is representative of his age. He is a prudent, bourgeois man who hoards things, draws up inventories and derives joy from seeing "all my goods in such order and . . . my stock of all necessaries so great" – more a grocer than an adventurer.

He is impulsive, superstitious, moody, an amateur philosopher. At times he imagines himself "king and lord of this country", at others he is humble and self-effacing to a degree. Any heroism lies in his dogged determination to survive every calamity.

Man Friday is "a comely handsome fellow, perfectly well made", the epitome of loyalty, companionship and obedience. In debate with Crusoe he displays wit and intelligence, courage and vivacity. Yet to Crusoe, Friday is never more than the best of servants, learning the white man's supposedly superior way of life and his subservience to a superior god. The first word of English Friday is taught is 'Master'.

A DISSENTING VOICE

Despite, or because of, a late start at writing, Defoe rushed into print – breathlessly and carelessly at times, but with an energetic passion, whether for a cause or for a character.

Daniel Defoe published his first major work at the relatively late age of 37. Writing with extraordinary speed and fluency he poured out verse, journalism, tracts and pamphlets, biographies and books of voyages, often mingling fact with fiction, and concealing his identity under pseudonyms, to the confusion of later researchers. A recent but by no means final estimate puts the number of Defoe's works at about 560. For most readers, however, he is the author of half a dozen narratives, composed in his old age, which helped to lay the foundations for the English novel.

POLITICS AND PROPAGANDA

In his prime, Defoe was not famous as a novelist; he was famous as a pamphleteer in an era rich with talent in the field. He was deemed greater than Swift or any other contemporary. Defoe's speciality was the cause of the Dissenter (he published 65 works on the subject) and attacking the Jacobites and the Catholic Church. But he wrote also about elections, wars, duels, trade, the Press, public health, the colonies and servants. He stooped frequently to raw insult and slander, especially in reference to the Pope. But in an age when readers liked being harangued and having their emotions whipped up, it was hugely welcome.

Poetry, too, was a largely political sport in Defoe's days. It generally concerned itself with celebrating great men, events and political parties – it was, in short, propaganda. But it was propaganda that found an appreciative audience. Defoe's *True-Born Englishman* (1700), in support of the Dutch King William III's right to the English throne, ran to 10 legal editions in the first year and at least 12 pirated ones – and ultimately 50 editions in 50 years. For all its prosaic purpose, this kind of poetry was marked by grandiose rhetoric and biblical allusions. Defoe was very good at it, though he considered prose an easier option.

Many prose fictions had been written before Defoe's time, including chivalric romances, 'picaresque' tales of wandering and roguery, allegories, fables and fairy tales. But Defoe's novels differed from all of these in being narratives of plausible events taking place in the real world, experienced by credible, unexceptional people. The creation of this tradition was his great achievement. Moll Flanders and

Mansell Collection

A DIALOGUE BETWEEN A DISSENTER AND THE OBSERVATOR, CONCERNING The Shortest Way with the Dissenters.

LONDON, Printed in the Year, MDCCIII.

1

Mansell Collection

Documenting the Plague Year
In 1721 plague ravaged Europe. The Government took radical, unpopular measures to stop it crossing the Channel, and may have commissioned Defoe's book to help justify their actions. He adopted such a documentary style that his Journal of the Plague Year *was readily mistaken for an eye-witness account of the English plague of 1665 (below). He did, of course, have access to the chilling statistics and records of that time (right).*

Pilloried

Sentenced to stand in the pillory for writing a subversive tract (far left), Defoe wrote his famous A Hymn to the Pillory. *It was published and widely circulated before sentence was carried out, and by the time Defoe had to face his ordeal (people were actually killed in the pillory), the public was more disposed to cheer than stone him. He had become a popular hero (left).*

story but a history', describing the way in which the manuscript of *Memoirs of a Cavalier* supposedly came to light, and even writing a pseudonymous preface to his own *The King of Pirates* in which he discussed its authenticity.

While composing, he made extensive use of memoirs, travel books and other sources, using his powers of synthesis and imagination to produce works such as *A Journal of the Plague Year,* which has often been taken to be an eye-witness account of 1665. *Memoirs of a Cavalier* was so convincing that 18th-century historians 'identified' the author as a Colonel Andrew Newport, and the late 19th-century *Dictionary of National Biography* devotes an entry to Captain Charles Johnson, known only for his authoritative *History of the Most Notorious Pirates* – which is now generally agreed to have been written by Defoe. One of his contemporaries meant to insult Defoe by asserting that he was the master of only one 'little art', that of 'forging a story, and imposing it on the world for truth'.

FIRST-PERSON NARRATOR

Defoe used several techniques to convey authenticity. The narrative is almost always written in the first person, and is in effect a life-story of the principal character. This makes for vividness and immediacy, but requires exceptional powers of identification on the part of the writer, who must respond to events all through the novel from a point of view (and past experience) different from his own. Defoe's imaginative sympathy was such that he could write with equal plausibility in the characters of seafarer, cavalier, criminal and whore. His willingness to assume the persona of a woman – and a disreputable one at that – is one remarkable aspect of his genius.

Roxana live in society, face up to its worst hazard – poverty – and cope with it in a practical, matter-of-fact, amoral fashion. And although placed in an extreme situation, Robinson Crusoe comes through by

prosaic means – muskets, nails, seeds – and solid virtues such as hard work and perseverance.

Ironically, Defoe, like many of his contemporaries, was either uneasy about the propriety of writing fiction, or else failed to realize that his audience would willingly read a story that was 'not true'. For he made every possible effort to persuade readers his narratives were authentic reports, claiming that *Roxana* was 'not a

In praise of William

William III, who arrived in England in 1688 (right), stood for everything Defoe believed in: religious tolerance, moderate politics and the expansion of English trade. Defoe wittily defended his monarch in a best-selling poem, The True-Born Englishman.

Hogarth: The Stagecoach. Ashmolean Museum, Oxford

Island tour
*As well as visiting
Spain, Holland and
Italy, Defoe rode the
length of Britain
on horseback, making
business contacts. He
put his observations
and experiences into a
guide-book, giving
invaluable insights
into contemporary life
(right).*

Robinson Crusoe
*At the age of 59
Defoe discovered a
new talent – for
fiction. The work
which guaranteed his
immortality was a
supposedly auto-
biographical account
of a ship-wrecked
mariner (below).*

THE
LIFE
AND
STRANGE SURPRIZING
ADVENTURES
OF
ROBINSON CRUSOE,
Of YORK MARINER:
Who lived Eight and Twenty Years,
all alone in an un-inhabited Island on the
Coast of AMERICA, near the Mouth of
the Great River of OROONOQUE;
Having been cast on Shore by Shipwreck, where-
in all the Men perished but himself.
WITH
An Account how he was at last as strangely deli-
ver'd by PIRATES.
Written by Himself.
LONDON:
Printed for W. TAYLOR at the Ship in Pater-Noster
Row. MDCCXIX.

Mansell Collection

THE HANDWRITING OF DEFOE

A steady hand
*A sample of Defoe's handwriting (above)
demonstrates the easy fluency with which he
wrote – though with so many creditors at his
door, revision would have seemed an
unaffordable luxury.*

Defoe's style was superbly adapted to his purpose. His lack of a university education – closed to all Dissenters – may have been a positive advantage, helping him to avoid pretentious Latinate sentences and an over-use of erudite mythological references – although he was well acquainted with both Latin and the classics. He wrote plainly, drawing on a wide vocabulary but for the most part using everyday words.

The flowing, breathless quality of Defoe's writing probably reflects the pressure under which he worked. This may also account for its faults – repetitiveness and clumsiness, 'pointless' episodes, loose ends, occasionally bad sentence structure. It is just possible that some of these are deliberate mistakes, intended to help convince Defoe's readers that the narrator is not a practised writer. Yet with all his passion for verisimilitude, Defoe never removed the dozens of inconsistencies that occur in his novels. For example, having left his parrot on the island, Robinson Crusoe boards the ship that has rescued him – and the parrot is with him; and the *Memoirs of a Cavalier*, supposedly discovered after the battle of Worcester (1651), contains references to events after the King's restoration (1660); and so on.

The most plausible explanation seems to be that Defoe wrote so fast and published so quickly – presumably to get money – that he had no opportunity to revise his work. Later in life he admitted, 'I must beg my reader's indulgence, being

the most immethodical writer imaginable. It is true I lay down a scheme, but my fancy is so fertile I often start fresh hints, and cannot but pursue them.'

A STRANGE MORALITY

Consciously, Defoe wrote as a moralist. 'The fable is always made for the moral, not the moral for the fable', he asserts in the preface to *Moll Flanders*. But to modern eyes the moral lesson is applied in a suspiciously perfunctory fashion: in the last few paragraphs the sinner repents and settles down to a prosperous old age. Defoe's avowed intent may have been moral, but in the world as he actually describes it, morals are less important than money. His principal characters are not motivated by religion, love or ambition, but by the need and determination to survive, usually outside or on the margins of society. With the exception of Crusoe, they all find that their worst enemy is poverty; and they all regard it as axiomatic that morals must yield to the need to get money. Indeed, Defoe makes both Moll Flanders and Roxana insist that they have never been attracted to sinning for its own sake: "the vice came in always at the door of necessity, not at the door of inclination" – although, once begun, Moll continues as a thief, and Roxana as a whore, out of avarice and vanity.

Never before had such people been singled out to 'tell their stories', free of condemnation or any moralistic motives. Here was real literary innovation.

Defoe turned to fiction late. The first part of his *Robinson Crusoe* appeared in 1719 and ran to four editions in the same year. After this encouraging reception, books poured from Defoe's pen. *Memoirs of a Cavalier* (1720) has been hailed as the first English historical novel. *Captain Singleton,* which appeared only a few days later, is a narrative of travel and piracy. In *Moll Flanders* (1722) he writes in the character of a tough, warm-hearted woman, while *A Journal of the Plague Year* (1722) can best be described as a documentary historical novel. *Roxana* (1724), the memoirs of an internationally successful courtesan, is another imaginative coup. A *Tour through the Whole Island of Great Britain* (1724-26) remained an indispensable guidebook 50 years after publication, and still captures the flavour and sights of the age.

CAPTAIN SINGLETON

→ 1720 →

Mutiny aboard a man-of-war (right) begins Robert Singleton's career as a pirate. He and his fellow mutineers are shipwrecked on the island of Madagascar. Singleton manages to reach the African mainland and returns to England with a fortune in gold dust. When his wealth runs out, he returns to sea as a pirate. The shipboard companionship of a Quaker pirate, William Walters, makes Singleton increasingly aware of his sins and crimes, and the two men eventually resolve to attempt a break with their pirate confederates . . .

MEMOIRS OF A CAVALIER

→ 1720 →

A young English gentleman (below) is the unnamed narrator of this 'Military Journal of the Wars in Germany and the Wars in England'. He crosses to the Continent in 1630, and fights for the Holy Roman Emperor in the Thirty Years War. After witnessing the horrific sacking of Magdeburg, he changes sides and joins the Swedish army of King Gustavus Adolphus. Later, after the King's death, the narrator returns to England where he sides with Charles I in the Civil War and sees the final defeat of the Cavaliers at Naseby. Supposedly these 'memoirs' had been found among papers looted from the Royalists.

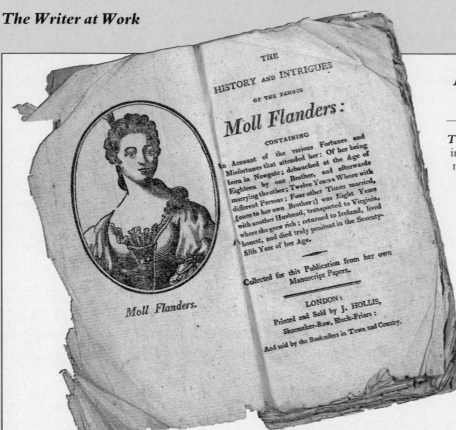

THE
HISTORY AND INTRIGUES
OF THE FAMOUS
Moll Flanders:

CONTAINING

An Account of the various Fortunes and Misfortunes that attended her: Of her being born in Newgate; debauched at the Age of Eighteen by one Brother, and afterwards marrying the other; Twelve Years a Whore with different Persons; Four other Times married, (once to her own Brother;) was Eight Years with another Husband, transported to Virginia, where she grew rich; returned to Ireland, lived honest, and died truly penitent in the Seventy-fifth Year of her Age.

Collected for this Publication from her own Manuscript Papers.

LONDON:
Printed and Sold by J. HOLLIS,
Shoemaker-Row, Black-Friars:

And sold by the Booksellers in Town and Country.

Moll Flanders.

A JOURNAL OF THE PLAGUE YEAR

→ 1722 ←

The horrific events (right) recorded in the supposed journal of H.F. the merchant are so convincing that many have taken it for a historical account rather than a novel.

Towards the end of 1664, two men die in Long Acre, and, with mounting terror, the citizens of London realise that 'the Great Visitation' is upon them. As the death toll rises, infected houses are shut up (with healthy as well as sick inside) and public gatherings are banned. Carts go through the streets collecting corpses to be buried in mass graves. H.F. mixes 'eye-witness' accounts with bills of mortality, statistics, musings on the impact on trade and prices, and philosophical debate.

Mansell Collection

MOLL FLANDERS

→ 1722 ←

One of Defoe's most vital and resilient characters, Moll Flanders (above) has an eventful life story to tell. Abandoned by her mother, she is brought up in the house of the mayor of Colchester. She is seduced by the elder son and married off to the younger, but he is only the first of five husbands. One is a spendthrift; another is her half-brother; the engaging Jemmy is a highwayman whom she leaves with regret in order to marry a banker. On his death, poor and no longer young, Moll turns to crime, becoming an accomplished pickpocket. Although she is finally caught, her adventures are far from over when Newgate Prison's doors clang shut.

A TOUR THROUGH THE WHOLE ISLAND OF GREAT BRITAIN

→ 1724-26 ←

Defoe's **Tour** *is both a survey and a lively guide,* 'particulary fitted for the reading of such as desire to travel over the ISLAND' (right). The material is based on his activities over several decades as merchant, spy and journalist, and packs in customs, antiquities, legends, houses, churches, gaols and hospitals, natural wonders and – Defoe's major preoccupation – the state of local trade.

Organized as a series of 'Circuits or Journies' over England, Scotland and Wales, this is a definitive portrait of early 18th-century Britain, thanks to Defoe's varied experience and artistry as a journalist.

ROXANA, OR THE FORTUNATE MISTRESS

→ 1724 ←

The daughter of French Protestant refugees, Mademoiselle de Beleau (right) is married at 15 to a London brewer. But in eight years "this thing called a husband" – a fool and a spendthrift – runs through her dowry and abandons her and her five children. She is soon destitute but, aided by her resourceful maid Amy, she acts with resolution. The children are settled with relatives, and Roxana (who narrates her own story) becomes a courtesan – a highly successful, wealthy one, known as the Countess Wintselsheim in Germany and the Lady Roxana in England.

Eventually, she marries a Dutch merchant who is unaware of her past, and at last she seems to have achieved secure wealth and respectability. Then one of her long-abandoned daughters discovers her relationship with this eminent, society figure, and determines that her mother shall acknowledge her. Roxana dreads exposure, but it is the maid Amy who – all-too-faithful – solves the problem in a drastic, terrible fashion.

Pirates and Buccaneers

The public attitude to piracy was a mixture of horror and admiration – not surprisingly, for the State rewarded 'useful' privateers while ruthlessly hunting down common pirates.

Daniel Defoe knew his readers well when he allowed Robinson Crusoe to be captured by pirates and when he made a notorious pirate the hero of his adventure story *Captain Singleton*. Pirates may have been criminals and cut-throats, rascals and robbers, but the public could hardly hear enough of them. Tales of their daring deeds and adventures on the high seas – not to mention their more grisly exploits – were the very stuff of alehouse gossip and speculation, and the execution of a pirate was a public event guaranteed to draw a large crowd. Piracy was in its heyday at the time Defoe was writing *Robinson Crusoe*. Only the year before the terrible 'Blackbeard' had died in hand-to-hand combat.

Rumour has it that Defoe knew some of the pirates personally; he was certainly fascinated by them. In his *The King of Pirates*, Defoe wrote a detailed factual account of the exploits of Captain John Avery, a notorious pirate and self-styled 'King of Madagascar'. And Defoe was probably the author of *A General History of the Robberies . . . of the Most Notorious Pirates* (1724) under the pseudonym of Captain Charles Johnson. This lively report on the most infamous pirates of the day is so detailed and accurate that it seems it could only have been written from first-hand knowledge. But whether Defoe knew any pirates or not, he could not fail to hear stories of their exploits.

The pirate hero dated back to the days of Sir Francis Drake and other Elizabethan adventurers who preyed upon Spanish merchant vessels, homeward-bound from the Spanish colonies in the Americas, laden with treasure. The bitter rivalry between Spain and England made men such as Drake heroes back home. Meanwhile the 'unfair' restrictions the Spaniards placed upon their colonies, forbidding them to trade with the

Colonies of pirates
The English colony of Jamaica was in fact a nest of pirates. But when Spain threatened to reclaim it, Henry Morgan made an 'authorized' rout of Puerto del Principe (left).

A ready market
Ports such as Bristol (above) provided a market place for plunder from piracy in the West Indies. It was also a recruiting ground for pirate crews and slave traders. Pirates were often considered local heroes.

'King of Buccaneers'
Based in Jamaica, Henry Morgan (left) organized semi-official, murderous raids on Spanish towns and ships. He extorted and looted a fortune. For this he was rewarded with a knighthood and made Lieutenant-Governor of Jamaica.

IUAN MORGAN

Mansell Collection

Mary Evans Picture Library

Anon: Bristol Docks and Quay/Bristol City Art Gallery/Bridgeman Art Library

victims, caring little whether targets were 'legitimate' or not.

The Spaniards naturally objected, and every now and then the French and English governments would shake their heads disapprovingly – and do nothing. Indeed, far from discouraging the activities of the buccaneers, they often made use of their services. More than once, the notorious Henry Morgan was employed by the English authorities in raids on Spanish colonies – and was rewarded with a knighthood and official post. Of course, even with the will to do so, the authorities would have found it hard to stop the buccaneers, for they operated in distant waters far beyond the reach of the law.

ROAMING THE SEVEN SEAS

At first, the buccaneers operated prinicpally in the Caribbean. But as the century wore on, they ventured further and further afield and hunted after Spanish prey on all the Seven Seas. A few sailed right around the world.

Though buccaneers were little more than gangsters, many were also skilled and brave seamen, and soon tales of their daring exploits began to filter back home. By the end of the century, racy accounts of voyages by such brave buccaneers as William Dampier, Basil Ringrose and Lionel Wafer made gripping, and highly popular, reading and were an inspiration to Defoe.

Yet by the 1690s, the mask of legitimacy was beginning to slip. Buccaneering degenerated into piracy – and not just in the Caribbean, where the outbreak of war in Europe in 1689 had forced the

merchants of any other nation, gave piratical activities a kind of legitimacy in the eyes of the world. The English government never officially condoned such actions, but it was quite happy to see the Spaniards harried, and to then collect its share of the spoils.

Yet it was the buccaneers – the English, French and Dutch sea rovers who terrorized the Caribbean and Pacific in the 17th century – who were the true begetters of the piratic tradition. These swashbuckling 'Brethren of the Coast' claimed a dubious legal status from the 'letters of marque' they carried. But in reality they were little more than pirates – they just chose to plunder and pillage only Spanish ships.

Swooping on poorly protected merchant vessels and colony settlements, these little bands of marauders became the scourge of the Spaniards from the 1630s onwards. Sometimes they operated in a 'gentlemanly' fashion, suavely taking their booty and leaving their victims empty-handed but little the worse for their experience. But more often, they tortured and terrorized their

Defoe's Blackbeard
"The lieutenant caused Blackbeard's head to be severed from his body and hung up at the bowsprit's end" (right). Among other anecdotes about Edward 'Blackbeard' Teach, Defoe tells in his General History of the Pirates *that it took 25 wounds – five of them from pistol-shots – to kill him; that he built a 'practice' hell in the hold using brimstone; that he had 14 wives; and that his crew included a nameless man believed to be the Devil.*

Fotomas

buccaneers to choose between fighting for their country or freebooting. Pirates began to flourish as never before, taking rich pickings from Europe's rapidly expanding colonial trade. In those days, no European powers had navies capable of policing seas so far from home.

Pirates were recruited from many walks of life. Some were discharged soldiers with nothing else to do; some were servants on the run, or deserters, or mutineers; some were escaping from poverty; and some were just bored young men looking for adventure. They were always armed, for life as a pirate was brutal and dangerous. Tradition pictures them sailing under their famous flag the 'Jolly Roger', or the 'skull and crossbones', but there were others: skeletons with headscarves and blood-dripping swords, for example. Pirate ships were given expressive names – *Defiance, Revenge, Happy Deliverance* – as were the pirates: 'Blackbeard', 'Gentleman Harry', 'Calico Jack'.

DANGERS ON BOARD

Ships were crowded and cramped, and men slept on the open decks or in the hold which was dark, stuffy and extremely hot. Water was the only drink, unless rum and brandy had been purloined from a captured ship, and on a long voyage food often ran short, and scurvy was rife.

During the voyage the crew was constantly on the look-out, for the first man to spy a prize could claim a large share of the booty. Once a ship was sighted, the pirate ship was made ready for action, and brought alongside to board her. If the prize was a good one, the pirates might change over from their own ship, after setting fire to it.

Heroes or barbarians?
When measures were taken in the 17th century to curtail the nefarious activities of pirates (right), two major obstacles arose. England, France and Spain all had policies forbidding colonials to buy goods other than from the mother country. This restraint on trade made cheap, smuggled goods highly saleable in the colonies. The other disadvantage was the strong appeal piracy had for the public imagination. Piratical exploits were guaranteed to horrify, titillate and fascinate such people as Defoe and his readers. Amnesties granted during the reigns of Charles I and II and George I resulted in many surrenders, but penitent pirates had a way of returning to their former trade when their money ran out.

Cherished myths
All the elements now associated with swashbuckling pirate fiction – the Jolly Roger, the treasure map, the buried pieces-of-eight (left) – have foundations in truth. The map pictured far left is that of pirate-captain William Read, dating from about 1819. Defoe recounts how Blackbeard, on the night before he died, was asked "whether his wife knew where he had buried his money? He answered, That nobody but himself and the Devil knew where it was, and the longest liver should take all."

Mary Evans Picture Library

After Rossel: Engagement between two vessels/Musée de la Marine/Bridgeman Art Library

governor of Virginia sent an expedition to hunt him down. Blackbeard met his death in 1718, when, lured on board a navy ship, he engaged in a long and savage hand-to-hand combat with the naval commander Robert Mayward.

Another notorious pirate was Captain John Avery, known as 'Long Ben', the subject of Defoe's book *The King of Pirates*. Born in Plymouth in 1665, Long Ben went to sea as a boy and soon rose to become mate on a merchant ship. But despairing of the continual hardships of the sailor's life, he incited the crew to mutiny against their drunken skipper. Steering his hijacked ship out of Corunna, Long Ben headed south. He proved a daring leader and, after many successes off the Guinea Coast and in the Caribbean, he sailed to India. There he seized a rich ship belonging to the Great Mogul (said to have aboard not only 100,000 pieces-of-eight but also the Mogul's daughter) and set himself up as King on Madagascar. (According to Defoe's account, however, Avery denied this.) Taking the name Bridgeman, he eventually returned to England, where he died in dire poverty.

The name of Captain William Kidd, who operated in waters as far apart as the West Indies and the Indian Ocean, has become synonymous with legends of buried treasure. In 1695 Kidd was commissioned to defend English ships in the Red Sea and the Indian Ocean. The voyage was dogged by disease, mutiny and failure. Only when Kidd was returning to the West Indies with the captive *Quedagh Merchant* did he learn that charges of piracy had been brought against him. He denied the charges, insisting he was a legitimate privateer, and returned to New York to clear himself. There he was arrested, taken to London, and, in 1701, convicted and hanged, protesting his innocence to the very last.

Piracy was very much a man's world, but two women also made names for themselves – Anne Bonney and Mary Read. As a child, Mary Read was a tomboy, always dressing in boys' clothing and playing rough games. As soon as she could,

A few pirates continued to believe their actions were justified, particularly at a time when the European nations were exploiting their colonies. The French Captain Misson flew a white flag of peace, bearing the legend 'For God and Liberty', and established a short-lived utopian-socialist settlement called Liberation on the island of Madagascar, where there was no private ownership or slavery.

However, the image which persisted in the public imagination was one of cruelty and barbarity. If half the tales are to be believed, pirates' victims would be whipped, beaten, made to walk the plank, dragged naked through infested swamps, burned, mutilated, made to eat their own flesh – or simply left to die. Back home, grisly details were relished and embellished. They had the same chill of excitement that horror films have today, mixing horror and daring adventure with a hint of the exotic.

Many of the pirates of the early 18th century became legends in their lifetime, famed for their bravery or brutality. Of them all, perhaps 'Blackbeard' was the most infamous. A large, sinister-looking man with a vast, bushy beard that reached to his waist, Edward 'Blackbeard' Teach was born in Bristol. His hunting-ground was the entire coast of North America. Eventually the

Surrender and die
There was little incentive for pirates to surrender (below), even against overwhelming odds. Except during a rare period of amnesty, they were certain to hang.

Mary Evans Picture Library

she ran away and, dressed as a man, joined a Dutch merchant ship which was captured by the notorious Captain Jack Rackham, or 'Calico Jack' as he was known. The pirate ship also contained another woman, Anne Bonney, common-law wife to Calico Jack. Anne Bonney fell in love with the disguised Mary and when Mary eventually revealed her identity, the two entered into partnership. Dressed in trousers and shirts and armed with pistols and cutlasses, they were every bit as blood-thirsty as their male colleagues. They were captured in 1720 and Mary died in prison; Anne's fate is unknown.

PURITANICAL PIRATE

Bartholomew Roberts was the last famous pirate and perhaps he was the greatest of them all. Born in Wales in 1682, he was a fanatical teetotaller who also abominated cards, dice, betting and 'loose women' – in total contrast to the majority of the Jolly Roger pirates. He was a dandy who dressed in magnificent plumed hats, bright scarves and costly weapons, and ran a highly disciplined ship. He died fighting in 1722 and is credited with having taken more than 400 ships.

Few pirates died of natural causes. Most came to a violent end, and were either killed in action or in quarrels with their comrades. Disease and alcohol abuse also took their toll. Once sentenced, pirates were taken to the dreaded Newgate Prison and then, in the execution cart, to Wapping, where their arrival was greeted by yells and cheers from the mob. Many went to their death with as much bravado as they had displayed in living, playing to the crowd with a humorous or defiant final speech. Corpses of the most important pirates were embalmed in tar and hung up in chains to serve as a warning to others.

Mary Evans Picture Library

Sentenced to hang
Outlawed by society, pirates often ended their days in violence, disease or on the gallows (above).

Women pirates
Anne Bonney and Mary Read (below) rivalled their male colleagues in cruelty.

Swashbuckling heroes
The allure of piracy lives on, glamorized and popularized by the silver screen (below).

Mary Evans Picture Library

Warner Bros./Kobal Collection

SIR WALTER SCOTT

← *1771-1832* →

A romantic as well as a realist, Sir Walter Scott had a lifelong passion for Scotland's dramatic history, which he poured into his poetry and prose. His seemingly effortless ability to relive the past made him – almost by accident – a pioneer of the historical novel, and a writer of incalculable influence on such diverse novelists as the Brontës, George Eliot and Leo Tolstoy. His literary fame was coupled with immense personal popularity, and at his death he was designated by the historian Thomas Carlyle as the 'pride of all Scotchmen'.

'Wizard of the North'

The most famous and revered Scotsman of his time, Scott acquired a renown for his extraordinary literary achievements that reached far beyond the borders of his native country.

In Princes Street, the main thoroughfare of Edinburgh, stands a monument to Sir Walter Scott, towering 200 feet high. Few British writers have been so conspicuously honoured in their native city. But the tribute is not excessive – it is a testimony to the enormous influence Scott exerted, both as a writer and as a popularizer of his country's history, traditions and landscape.

Walter Scott was born in Edinburgh on 15 August 1771. On both sides of the family he was descended from ancient Border yeoman families. His father, also named Walter Scott, was the first member of his family to live in a town and adopt a profession – he was a respected solicitor (attorney). Scott's mother, Anne Rutherford, was the daughter of a professor of medicine at Edinburgh University. From his father, Walter inherited his attitude to work, and from his mother his imaginative gifts.

CRIPPLED IN CHILDHOOD

Walter was the fourth of six surviving children. When he was a baby the family moved from Edinburgh's picturesque but dirty Old Town to the much healthier New Town – an area of splendid contemporary Georgian buildings. Despite the beneficial move, Walter, while still a toddler, was struck by an illness (probably poliomyelitis) that left his right leg permanently lame. He was therefore sent to live at his paternal grandfather's farmhouse at Sandy-Knowe in the country air of the Border moorlands. Various remedies were tried to cure his lameness, and one of his earliest memories was of lying on his grandfather's parlour floor, wrapped in the skin of a newly killed sheep.

His disability remained, but young Walter grew up strong and vigorous in all other ways. One of his greatest pleasures was listening to the tales of Border history and legend that the old folks told. His memory for these tales was phenomenal, and this early period at his grandfather's house had a strong influence in nurturing his vivid historical imagination.

In 1778, Walter entered the High School in Edinburgh, where he acquired a proficiency in Latin and modern languages that was directly inspired by his desire to read stories and poems in these languages. Naturally high-spirited and outgoing, he quickly made himself popular with the other boys with his inexhaustible gift for storytelling. This popularity was to last throughout his life – indeed, he came to be loved and admired by virtually everyone he met, from royalty to peasants.

Walter spent six months at Kelso Grammar School before proceeding to Edinburgh University at the age of 12 – then not unusually young. Like many students, he did not read for a degree, but simply attended classes

in which he was interested. However, his studies were interrupted by a serious illness, described by his later son-in-law and biographer, John Gibson Lockhart, as 'the bursting of a blood vessel in the lower bowels'.

After his convalescence (during which he was forbidden to speak), young Scott embarked on a five-year legal apprenticeship to his father. He later said he would have become a soldier if he had not been lame; instead he submitted to 'the dry and barren wilderness of forms and conveyances'. Unlike his father, he decided to become an advocate (counselor-at-law or barrister) and in 1792 was admitted to the Bar.

Although Scott's heart was not in the Law, he made a living at it, and found that life as a young advocate had many pleasant aspects. He travelled considerably around his native countryside and so added to his knowledge of Scottish history, folklore and traditions. When he was 24 he became curator of the Advocates' Library, where he spent many happy hours in the study

Old Town, New Town
(right) Edinburgh in the late 18th and early 19th centuries was one of the most cultivated cities in Europe, and many splendid buildings were constructed in Scott's lifetime. This view shows Princes Street in 1825 (where Scott's monument now stands). On the right is the Old Town with its tightly packed buildings; on the left the regular facades of Princes Street mark the edge of the spaciously laid out Georgian New Town.

By kind permission of Mrs. Maxwell-Scott, Abbotsford

A varied childhood
(above and right) Scott was born in this street of rather ramshackle houses, but by the time he was six (when the portrait above was painted) he had moved several times – first to the New Town, then to his grandfather's Border farmhouse, and then to Bath, where he spent a year with an aunt in the hope – which unfortunately was not realized – of curing his lameness. When Scott was six, the writer Alicia Cockburn called him 'the most extraordinary genius of a boy I ever saw'.

Scottish National Portrait Gallery

Alexander Nasmyth: Princess Street. Private Collection/Phaidon Press

of old documents. His busy social life included membership of literary and debating societies, and in 1792 he joined a German class in order to read German Romantic literature. His enthusiasm bore fruit in his first book, a translation of some German poems which was published anonymously in 1796.

A HAPPY MARRIAGE

At this time, Scott was also experiencing the pleasures and pains of love. In the early 1790s he was smitten by Williamina Belsches, who was from a higher social class than he, but seemed to return his affections. In 1796, however, she married a rich young banker, and Scott said that although he could put together the pieces of his broken heart, 'the crack will remain to my dying day'. He did, indeed, remember his first love all his life, but the next year he not only fell for another woman, but married her. She was Charlotte Carpenter or Charpentier, who had been born in France but brought to England as a girl. Their relationship was companionable rather than passionate – 'it was something short of love in all its fervour', he wrote – but it apparently made for a very happy marriage.

In 1799 Scott's father died, leaving a sizeable legacy to each of his children, and the same year Scott was appointed Sheriff-Depute of Selkirkshire, a post which paid £300 a year in return for fairly light duties. The improvement in his financial circumstances allowed

By kind permission of Mrs. Maxwell-Scott, Abbotsford

Parental influence

Scott's solicitor father was a formal and temperate man, but he was also kind-hearted and extraordinarily scrupulous in his business dealings. Scott, who inherited his father's integrity and concern for others, said 'He had a zeal for his clients which was almost ludicrous'. Scott's mother was privately educated to be 'well-bred in society', and her son also grew up to be at ease in any company.

Laird of Abbotsford

(above and right) Scott loved his life as a country gentleman at his beautiful Abbotsford estate (above). A most generous host to his many guests, he was also extremely popular with the local people. In this painting (right) by the leading Scottish artist Sir David Wilkie, Scott has had himself and his family depicted as a group of peasants. Scott was devoted to his dogs, and frequently, as here, they appear in portraits with him.

him to devote more time to writing, and in 1802-3 he published to great acclaim his first major work, the three-volume *Minstrelsy of the Scottish Border*.

Meanwhile, the war with Napoleon's France had sparked off fears of an invasion, and in 1797 Scott joined the Royal Edinburgh Volunteer Light Dragoons. He became 'Paymaster, Quartermaster and Secretary' and took part in drilling and exercises, for although he was lame, his strength was such that he could walk 30 miles a day and he was an excellent horseman.

His military exploits, however, were not appreciated by the Lord Lieutenant of Selkirkshire, who thought that Scott was devoting too much of his time to soldiering and invoked an old rule that the Sheriff-Depute of the county should live within the area of his jurisdiction for at least four months of the year. So in 1804 Scott rented a house called Ashestiel, a few miles from Selkirk and pleasantly situated on the Tweed. By this time he had two daughters and a son; a second son, born in the following year, completed the family.

Scott's work in editing medieval romances encouraged him to try a similar type of composition himself, and in 1805 he published a long narrative poem, *The Lay of the Last Minstrel*, set in the 16th century and based on a Border legend of a goblin. This, his first important original literary work, was an immediate success, running to five editions in a year. In the next few years Scott published several other best-selling poems in the same vein, notably *Marmion* and *The Lady of the Lake*. The latter engendered a rush of interest in Loch Katrine, the setting of the poem.

Scott was prospering in other ways. In 1804 an uncle left him some property which he sold for £5000, and in 1806 he was appointed a Clerk of Session, an important official in Scotland's supreme civil court. The duties

Scotland's tourist image

(right) Virtually single-handed, Scott created the glamorous public image of Scotland's history and landscape, and in so doing he gave birth to Scotland's tourist industry. The Edinburgh publisher Robert Cadell described the 'extraordinary sensation' caused by Scott's poem The Lady of the Lake *(1810), which is set at Loch Katrine (right). 'The whole country rang with the praises of the poet – crowds set off to the scenery of Loch Katrine, till then comparatively unknown; and as the book came out just before the season for excursions, every home in that neighbourhood was crammed with a constant succession of visitors.'*

carried a salary of £1300 a year but were not too arduous, and Scott often used his time in court to catch up with correspondence (he was even accused of writing his books in court, but he denied this).

In 1811, Scott bought a farmhouse on the Tweed. The site was originally called Clarty Hole, but he renamed it, more romantically, Abbotsford. This was to be his home for the rest of his life, although he had to spend a good part of the year in Edinburgh because of his court duties. He bought neighbouring land to create an estate and built up a palatial country house, complete with a large library. Scott realized that, even with his sheriffship and clerkship, he needed to keep up a prolific literary output to finance Abbotsford, and he continued to pour out narrative verse. In 1813 he was offered, but declined, the poet laureateship.

A CHANGE OF DIRECTION

That same year, quite by chance, the direction of his career changed completely. According to Scott's own account, he was searching for some fishing tackle in a drawer when he came across the manuscript of a novel he had begun eight years earlier. He had laid it aside then, because of adverse comments by a friend whose judgement he valued. But Scott decided to complete it, and, warming to his task, he wrote the last two-thirds during the evenings of three weeks. The book was *Waverley*, which on its publication in 1814 proved even

By kind permission of Mrs. Maxwell-Scott, Abbotsford

Companion and wife
Charlotte Carpenter or Charpentier married Scott in 1797. He said that their love increased with the years, but he never forgot his first, lost love, and his marriage 'was something short of love in all its fervour which I suspect people only feel once in their lives'.

more successful than *The Lady of the Lake*, and marked the beginning of one of the most remarkable sequences of novels in English literature.

The book was published anonymously, and its successors always carried on the title page the words 'by the author of Waverley'. Various explanations have been suggested as to why Scott wanted to keep his authorship secret – one being that the novelist's 'lowly' status conflicted with his dignity as an important legal official. Another factor is that speculation about the identity of 'the Great Unknown' kept interest in the books alive and boosted sales. In literary circles Scott's secret was an open one. In the year that *Waverley* was published, Jane Austen wrote: 'Walter Scott has no business to write novels, especially good ones. It is not fair. He has Fame and Profit enough as a Poet . . .' Yet to outsiders it seemed scarcely credible that someone who already had an extraordinarily full business and social life could find time to write substantial novels at a rate of almost two a year.

Scott's method was to rise early in the morning and do several hours' work at his desk while the rest of the household slept. His many guests at Abbotsford, to whom he was the perfect host, never suspected the labours he accomplished before they came down to breakfast. Most of the 'Waverley Novels' dealt with Scottish history, so Scott already had much of the material in his head and wrote with astonishing

Alexander Fraser: Loch Katrine/Fine Art Photographic Library

(*Fact or Fiction*)

ROBIN HOOD

The first recorded mention of Robin Hood is in a 14th-century poem; later he became a popular figure in ballads. There is no firm evidence that such a man ever lived, but there is almost certainly some historical basis for the stories. In Scott's *Ivanhoe*, he appears as the honourable outlaw, Locksley, who opposes the upstart Norman Prince John.

Mansell Collection

Son-in-law biographer
The writer John Gibson Lockhart who, like Scott, was a lawyer by training, married Scott's daughter Sophia in 1820. This portrait of them was painted much later, in fact after Sophia was dead. Lockhart knew his father-in-law intimately and his extremely long, minutely detailed Life of Sir Walter Scott *is one of the classics of literary biography. Many critics rank it next to Boswell's* Life of Johnson.

fluency. An exception is *Ivanhoe*, the first of his novels with a purely English setting. Although he did not publicly acknowledge his authorship of the Waverley novels until 1827, Scott was by now the most famous living Scotsman. In 1820 he was made a baronet and in 1822 he supervised George IV's visit to Scotland.

Scott enjoyed his busy and energetic life to the full, and his happiness reached a peak in 1825 when his beloved elder son, also called Walter, married a pretty young heiress, Jane Jobson. 'There is gold in her garters', wrote Scott, and although his attitude was not really as mercenary as it sounds (he had a deep affection for her), the subject of money was always at the forefront of his mind. As 1825 drew to a close it was an increasing source of worry. His fortune was, in fact, built on very shaky foundations, and the next year it was to topple like a house of cards.

FINANCIAL RUIN

This extraordinary downfall can be explained by the complex nature of his literary dealings at a time when publishing was becoming 'big business' and fortunes could be made or lost overnight. Since 1805, Scott had been involved in publishing as more than an author, for he had gone into partnership with the printer James Ballantyne, an old school friend. Four years later he founded the firm of John Ballantyne and Company, booksellers and publishers, with James and his brother John. Both the printing and publishing sides of the business ran into financial trouble. Scott was able to steer business their way, but he also lost money for them by getting them to produce unsaleable antiquarian texts. They were rescued by another Edinburgh publisher, Archibald Constable, who from 1818 onwards issued Scott's novels.

The financial arrangements linking the Ballantynes, Constable and Scott became extremely involved, and Scott often spent money that he did not really have. He borrowed large sums and was in the habit of getting advances from Constable in the form of post-dated bills of exchange, which he would immediately sell at a discount for cash. In December 1825 Constable's London agents, Hurst Robinson & Co., went bankrupt, and in a chain reaction Constable and Ballantyne (and thus Scott himself) followed suit.

Scott had kept secret his involvement in publishing and when it suddenly became known that he was

ROBERT BURNS

Scott's greatest contemporary Scottish writer was Robert Burns (1759-96), who also had a great love for his country's heritage. They met only once, when Scott was 15. This painting records an earlier incident with young Scott gazing at Burns in an Edinburgh bookshop.

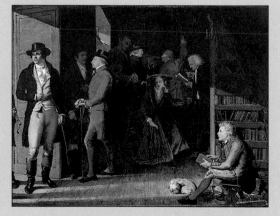

Royal pageantry

(left) Scott was one of the guests at the coronation of George IV in London on 19 July 1821. He wrote that it was 'impossible to conceive a ceremony more august and imposing in all its parts, and more calculated to make the deepest impression both on the eye and the feelings'. In the following year Scott was given the honour of organizing the ceremonials for the King's visit to Scotland.

A nation mourns

(below) Scott was so popular that his death caused widespread grief. His son-in-law Lockhart recorded that at his funeral at Dryburgh Abbey 'when the coffin was taken from the hearse, and again laid on the shoulders of the afflicted serving-men, one deep sob burst from a thousand lips.'

ruined – with personal debts of over £100,000 – his friends were shocked and dismayed. A group of them offered to lend him money, but with a magnificent resolve that would have done credit to any of his fictional heroes, Scott refused, saying 'No, this right hand shall work it all off!' He was allowed to keep Abbotsford and he settled down to a regime of work that was gruelling even by his standards. The death of his wife in 1826 was another bitter blow, but he worked on indomitably, and in the space of two years his writing paid off nearly £40,000 of his debts. His astonishing output included not only novels, but also a nine-volume biography of Napoleon.

As a result of the strain of such a workload, the quality of Scott's writing declined and his health began to give way. He had a stroke in 1831 and, in the hope of recovery, made an eight-month voyage to the Mediterranean. It is a mark of the esteem in which he was held that his ship was provided by the Government.

Scott had further strokes on the voyage and, realizing he was dying, could think of nothing but getting back to his beloved Scotland. His son-in-law Lockhart has movingly described the long journey home – how Scott, bemused and feeble though he was, rose in spirits as he recognized places he knew and murmured their names. He arrived back at Abbotsford on 11 July and died on 21 September 1832, with all his children at his bedside. 'It was so quiet a day', wrote Lockhart, 'that the sound he best loved, the gentle ripple of the Tweed over its pebbles, was distinctly audible as we knelt round the bed and his eldest son kissed and closed his eyes.'

Sir Walter Scott was buried at Dryburgh Abbey, a few miles from his home, and Lockhart records that the newspapers 'had the signs of mourning usual on the demise of a king'. His copyrights and remaining liabilities were taken over by the publisher Robert Cadell, who made a fortune from them. His beloved home, Abbotsford, however, passed to Scott's eldest son and still belongs to his direct descendants.

IVANHOE

In this chivalric romance, Scott conjures up a kaleidoscopic image of medieval England, where historical and imaginary characters cross swords both in love and war.

Although not the first to write historical novels, Scott emphatically established their popularity throughout Europe. Before *Ivanhoe*, he had set his novels in Scotland's recent past, a period he knew intimately. Fearing that he might 'wear out the public favour' if he continued to write only about Scotland, he decided on a change of setting and period.

It was a bold step to move from his home ground to 12th-century England, but Scott succeeded so well in portraying medieval life that even today, consciously or unconsciously, we tend to see the Middle Ages through his eyes. As the Victorian writer Walter Bagehot said, one of Scott's achievements is that he gives us 'the middle ages as we should have wished them to have been'.

GUIDE TO THE PLOT
Ivanhoe is set in the reign of Richard I, the 'Lionheart', and the story arises from the enmity between the Saxons and their Norman overlords. Cedric of Rotherwood, a Saxon nobleman of "fiery and resolute disposition", is devoted to the cause of restoring the Saxon monarchy, and wishes his ward, the "exquisitely fair" Lady Rowena, to marry Athelstane of Coningsburgh, who is, like her, of royal Saxon descent. Physically brave, but self-indulgent and indolent, Athelstane holds no charm for Rowena – she is in love with

Révoil: The Tournament. Musée des Beaux-Arts, Lyon

A royal insult
(right) The Norman and Saxon nobility take their places in the galleries to "obtain a fair view into the lists", where the tournament is to take place. Isaac the Jew and his daughter, Rebecca, cause a stir for 'presuming' to sit with some lesser Norman gentry. Prince John's attention is attracted by the commotion, and he is transfixed by the sight of Rebecca. On a whim, he imperiously orders a group of "Saxon churls" to "make room for my prince of usurers and his lovely daughter", thereby adding insult to the Saxons' ever-present sense of injury.

J. A. A. Atkinson: The Passage-of-Arms at Ashby. Victoria and Albert Museum/Bridgeman

Cedric's son, Wilfred of Ivanhoe, who loves her in return.

Although a proud Saxon, Ivanhoe is loyal to the Norman King Richard. So Cedric has banished him. Having fought valiantly in the Crusades in the Holy Land, Ivanhoe has found favour with King Richard, the mightiest warrior of his day. During Richard's absence from England, his brother, Prince John, a man of "dissolute audacity mingled with extreme haughtiness", plots to take over the English throne.

> *"Four generations had not sufficed to blend the hostile blood of the Normans and Anglo-Saxons, or to unite…two hostile races, one of which still felt the elation of triumph, while the other groaned under all the consequences of defeat."*

Ivanhoe and Richard return secretly to England, and in a great tournament at Ashby-de-la-Zouche they triumph over all opponents. Richard, disguised as the Black Knight, keeps his identity hidden, but Ivanhoe – the "Disinherited Knight" – is exposed:
When the helmet was removed, the well-formed, yet sun-burnt features of a young man of twenty-five were seen amidst a profusion of fair hair. His countenance was as pale as death, and marked in one or two places with streaks of blood.

"Glory to the brave!"
(left) At the Ashby-de-la-Zouche tournament, the Norman knights, led by Brian de Bois-Guilbert, challenge Saxon skill and strength. After routing all comers, Bois-Guilbert fights it out with the mysterious Disinherited Knight, until "saddle, horse and man rolled on the ground in a cloud of dust . . . [and] stung with madness he drew his sword and waved it in defiance of his conqueror" (below). The Disinherited Knight takes on the other Normans with equally devastating effect, and emerges with the day's honours.

Having been severely wounded in the combat, Ivanhoe is nursed by Rebecca, a beautiful and courageous Jewish girl, who falls in love with him; but because she is a member of a persecuted race, she has no illusions about him feeling the same for her.

Among the Norman knights whom Ivanhoe has defeated in the tournament are the two principal villains of the piece, Sir Reginald Front-de-Boeuf and Sir Brian de Bois-Guilbert, both ruthless allies of Prince John. After the tournament, they capture Cedric, Rowena, Athelstane, the wounded Ivanhoe, Rebecca and her father, the rich Jew, Isaac. They are all imprisoned in Front-de-Boeuf's grim castle at Torquilstone. Front-de-Boeuf threatens Isaac with torture, unless he pays a huge ransom; and Rebecca is subjected to the amorous advances of Bois-Guilbert, but resists with a "high and firm resolve". Bois-Guilbert's passion is only kindled the more, for, "being proud himself and high-spirited, [he] thought he had never beheld beauty so animated and so commanding".

Cedric's faithful jester, Wamba the Witless, has managed to escape capture by the Normans. With Cedric's doughty swineherd, Gurth, Wamba enlists the help of King Richard and the outlaw Locksley, who lead an assault on Front-de-Boeuf's castle. Ivanhoe, weak from his wounds, is unable to rise from his bed, so Rebecca describes the course of the battle to him, from her vantage-point at the window. Richard, still disguised as the Black Knight, carries all before him, fighting "as if there were twenty men's strength in his single

A gentle nurse
(above) After the tournament, Rebecca has the wounded Ivanhoe (now stripped of his disguise as the Disinherited Knight) carried to her lodgings. She promises to heal him in eight days for, she tells him, "Our nation . . . can cure wounds, though we deal not in inflicting them"; and she continues her care of him when they are held captive in Front-de-Boeuf's castle. Her gift for healing is coupled with a natural revulsion from bloodshed and violence, and despite her growing love for Ivanhoe, she passionately questions his addiction to war and "glory". Yet, for all her gentleness of spirit, she is to show herself as courageous as "the vainest Nazarene [Christian] maiden".

37

Rejected passion

(left) Imprisoned at Front-de-Boeuf's castle, Rebecca falls victim to Bois-Guilbert's impassioned attentions. But she spurns and defies him – "one foot nearer and I plunge myself over the precipice!"

The castle falls

(below) The Black Knight and his men storm the castle and overwhelm its defenders. In the confusion, Bois-Guilbert seizes Rebecca and gallops off with her.

Mansell Collection

arm". He and the Saxons capture the castle, and all the prisoners are freed, with the exception of Rebecca, whom Bois-Guilbert abducts. He takes her to Templestowe, the local seat of the Knights Templar, the order of knighthood to which he belongs.

Isaac goes to Templestowe to attempt to negotiate his daughter's release, but is scornfully ejected. His appearance unfortunately alerts the Grand Master of the Templars to the presence of a Jewish captive. "An ascetic bigot", the Grand Master is appalled that a Christian house should secrete a 'heathen', and one whom he presumes is "the paramour of a brother of the Order". He thinks that Bois-Guilbert must be bewitched and has Rebecca put on trial for sorcery.

Rebecca is condemned to be burned at the stake, but at Bois-Guilbert's secret prompting, she exercises her right to demand a champion to fight for her in trial by combat. Bois-

A feast in the forest

(below) The Black Knight is rescued from a band of traitorous Norman knights by Locksley (Robin Hood), Friar Tuck and their fellow outlaws. Now revealed as Richard, King of England, he joins them in a feast of ale and venison, in the forest. "The merry king, nothing heeding his dignity . . . laughed, quaffed, and jested among the jolly band", who, though outlaws, "now formed his court and his guard".

Mansell Collection

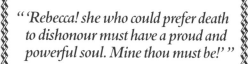

> "'Rebecca! she who could prefer death to dishonour must have a proud and powerful soul. Mine thou must be!'"

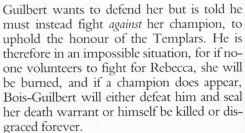

Guilbert wants to defend her but is told he must instead fight *against* her champion, to uphold the honour of the Templars. He is therefore in an impossible situation, for if no-one volunteers to fight for Rebecca, she will be burned, and if a champion does appear, Bois-Guilbert will either defeat him and seal her death warrant or himself be killed or disgraced forever.

Ivanhoe is Rebecca's most likely champion, but he is still in no condition to fight. Out of this brilliantly contrived situation, Scott brings his novel to a powerful and unexpected conclusion . . .

ACTION AND ADVENTURE

Ivanhoe is usually viewed first and foremost as a great adventure story. It was rapturously received by Scott's contemporaries, and one critic at least saw it as being addressed to 'that kind of boyish fancy which idolizes medieval society as the "fighting time"'. Scott certainly makes brilliant use of the colour and pageantry associated with medieval combat, and gives special prominence to the tournament at Ashby-de-la-Zouche and the highly dramatic siege of Torquilstone Castle.

Yet *Ivanhoe* is far from being a straightforward adventure yarn, and although Scott clearly relishes writing the action passages, his intention is not to glorify warfare. Indeed, he goes so far as to argue that heroic action, pursued to its conclusion, is ultimately self-defeating. Interestingly, he is able to express the fascination of outstanding military achievement, as well as the contradictory sentiments of anti-violence. He does this through the character of Rebecca, the true heroine of the book.

As she watches King Richard lead the attack on the castle where she and Ivanhoe are held captive, she cannot but admit that it is a breathtaking sight – "it is fearful, yet magnificent, to behold how the arm and heart of one man can triumph over hundreds". But she insists that triumph in battle is "an offering of sacrifice to the demon of vain glory" and asks Ivanhoe:

". . . is the rusted mail which hangs as a hatchment over the champion's dim and mouldering tomb, is the defaced sculpture of the inscription which the ignorant monk can hardly read to the inquiring pilgrim – are these sufficient rewards for the sacrifice of every kindly affection, for a life miserably spent that ye may make others miserable?"

A KING OF ILL REPUTE

King John, who succeeded his brother, Richard the Lionheart, in 1199, is one of the most unpopular of English monarchs. As Scott tells us, he plotted to take over the throne while Richard was at the Crusades – for which he was later banished. But despite John's reputation for cruelty and treachery, it has become clear that he was both cultured and a clever politician. At the end of his reign he was forced by rebellious barons to sign the Magna Carta, a charter of liberties – the most significant event of his 17-year rule.

British Library/Bridgeman Art Library

Despite differences in historical setting, *Ivanhoe* and the Scottish novels have a common theme – that of the strife arising from the conflict of cultures. There is an abiding hostility between the Saxons and the conquering Normans, which Scott explicitly chose to focus on, as he explains in his introduction. 'It seemed to the author that the existence of the two races in the same country, the vanquished distinguished by their plain, homely, blunt manners, and the free spirit infused by their ancient institutions and laws ... might interest the reader by contrast.'

PERSONAL CONFLICT
The contrast that Scott portrays is more subtle than this, however, for conflict arises not only from differences of background and outlook, but also from such human weakness as misplaced pride. Cedric, for example, is so blindly committed to his dream of restoring a Saxon king to the English throne that he is prepared to renounce his own son.

Scott further adds to the complexity of the issues by introducing 'other characters belonging to the same time and country' but of a different race – Rebecca and her father Isaac. As Jews they are despised by Norman and Saxon alike, but it is they, rather than the Christians, who freely display the 'Christian' virtues. Isaac is at times uncertain whether he loves money more than his daughter, but when put to the test he shows that he would be prepared to make any sacrifice for her. This is in sharp contrast to Cedric's treatment of Ivanhoe. And when Ivanhoe offers Rebecca money in return for her care of him she rejects it, asking only that he "believe henceforward that a Jew may do good service to a Christian, without desiring other guerdon [reward] than the blessing of the Great Father who made both Jew and Gentile."

Daniel Maclise: Robin Hood/Fine Art Photographic Library

CELEBRATING THE PAST

Sir Walter Scott 'invented' the modern historical novel. In a rapid succession of best-sellers, he brought to life the colourful, turbulent history of his own country, and that of neighbouring England.

Sir Walter Scott was the first British novelist to make a fortune by writing. The 'Waverley Novels' were tremendous best-sellers, composed at great speed and in rapid succession. In all, he wrote 27 novels in 18 years, and his enormous literary output also included tens of thousands of lines of poetry, a voluminous collection of ballads, massive editions of Dryden and Swift, a nine-volume biography of Napoleon, a three-volume child's history of Scotland, a long and fascinating *Journal*, and quantities of letters, reviews and stories.

Scott wrote fast, fluently and with a certain breezy carelessness that sometimes irritated critics. In the *Edinburgh Review*, the severe Francis Jeffrey praised *Waverley* almost in spite of himself: 'Here is a thing obviously very hastily, and, in many places, very unskilfully written . . . and yet, by the mere force, and truth, and vivacity of its colouring, already casting the whole tribe of ordinary novels in the shade.'

Scott worked best under pressure, with the printer almost waiting at his elbow. A passage from the *Journal*, itself hasty and under-punctuated, tells us that 'I love to have the press thumping, clattering and banging in my rear – it creates the necessity [which] almost always makes me work best – needs must when the Devil drives.'

Also driven on by his fertile imagination, Scott drew on his amazing memory and facility with language to create a succession of sprawling masterpieces, compelling stories as various and unshaped as life itself. He cheer-

Recreating the past *(left) Scott's home, Abbotsford, reflected the love of history which inspired his writing. He indulged his passion for the past almost to the point of bankruptcy – filling his rooms with a vast collection of armour, relics and curios. Surrounded by such images of the past, he set about creating his momentous series of historical novels – which he wrote in early morning, pre-breakfast sessions in his study (inset).*

Lucinda Lambton/Arcaid. Inset: By kind permission of Mrs. Maxwell-Scott, Abbotsford

fully admitted that, although he initially planned and plotted his books, they ran away with him:

'I think there is a demon who seats himself on the feather of my pen when I begin to write, and leads it astray from my purpose. Characters expand under my hand; incidents are multiplied . . . when I light on such a character as Bailie Jarvie [in *Rob Roy*], or Dalgetty [in *The Legend of Montrose*], my imagination brightens, and my conception becomes clearer at every step which I take in his company . . . If I resist the temptation . . . my thoughts become prosy, flat and dull . . . I am no more the same author . . . than the dog in a wheel, condemned to go round and round for hours, is like the dog merrily chasing his tail.'

'A WINNING GAME'

Money was an important incentive in Scott's writing. He denied that it was the main reason, though he declared himself 'not displeased to find the game a winning one'. His huge earnings financed the extravagances and generosity at Abbotsford which kept him always short of ready cash and eventually led

Historic landscapes
Scott's fascination with history was paralleled by his love of Scotland's landscape. Indeed, the two were associated in his mind: though time had passed since the old days, the landscape where historic events had happened remained unchanged – confirming a continuous link between past and present.

Rational historian
(above) The philosopher and historian David Hume (1711-76), a leading figure in Scotland's Enlightenment, wrote a massive History of Great Britain. *Scott was affected by the rational climate of the Enlightenment, but also delighted in the wilder times of Scotland's past.*

THE GREAT UNKNOWN
LATELY DISCOVERED IN IRELAND.

Although Scott was theoretically 'unknown', he was cheered through Dublin's streets in 1825.

to his bankruptcy. After this event, rapid and continuous literary production was more necessary than ever.

In spite of his success and his prodigious capacity for hard work, Scott's literary career was remarkably unplanned in its course. He was well into his 30s before he published a significant original literary work, *The Lay of the Last Minstrel*. Before then he had shown that even as an antiquarian scholar he had a golden touch, for his collection of old ballads, *The Minstrelsy of the Scottish Border* (1802-03) was a best-seller.

Chance played a part in the composition of *The Lay of the Last Minstrel*. The subject of the poem was suggested by the Countess of Dalkeith, who had heard a legend of a goblin called Gilpin Horner and thought it was ideal material for Scott. He jumped at the suggestion and set off on a series of poems that made him the forerunner of those 20th-century authors whose block-busters are fought over by publishers. *The Lay of the Last Minstrel* was such a runaway success that the publisher Constable offered Scott 1000 guineas for his next poem, *Marmion*, before he had seen a single line of it.

Scott realized he was not a great poet (he told his children not to waste their time reading his verse), but the fast movement, colour and romance of his work caught the public imagination. The stirring ballad *Lochinvar* that Scott included in *Marmion* is a good example. The poem tells with tremendous verve how the bold Lochinvar rescues his beloved Ellen as she is about to be married to a rival – 'a laggard in love and a dastard in war'. Lochinvar triumphantly carries her off on his horse:

So faithful in love and so dauntless in war,
There never was knight like the young Lochinvar.

Scott continued publishing long, narrative poems until 1817, but by then it was Lord Byron's poetry that was on everyone's lips. In comparison with Byron's melancholy, introspective heroes rebelling against conventional morality, Scott's characters seemed wooden and juvenile. His switch to novel-writing – though evidently accidental – came at an opportune moment and gave him a new outlet for his enormous, casual erudition in Scottish history and legend. It is clear that from boyhood he was a compulsive storyteller of 'old unhappy times'.

One of Scott's proclaimed motives for

The Jacobite Rebellion

The Battle of Culloden (1746), the final defeat of Bonnie Prince Charlie and his Jacobite rebels by the English troops under the 'Butcher' Duke of Cumberland (above), was a point in Scottish history which fascinated Scott. It focused his interest in the Jacobites – the supporters of the exiled Stuart Kings – who feature in some of his finest novels. He was first introduced to Jacobite tales and songs as a boy, and developed 'a very strong prejudice in favour of the Stuart family'. This prejudice increased when he heard about 'the cruelties exercised . . . in the Highlands, after the Battle of Culloden. One or two of our own distant relations had fallen on that occasion, and I remember detesting the name of Cumberland with more than infant hatred. Mr Curle . . . husband of one of my aunts, had been present at their execution; and it was probably from him that I first heard these tragic tales which made so great an impression on me'. In Waverley Scott was intent upon recreating the romance as well as the tragedy of the Highlanders' struggle in the 1745 Jacobite Rebellion. Rob Roy goes further back to the Jacobite Rebellion of 1715; and in Redgauntlet Scott mixed history with fantasy to write about the imagined return from exile of Bonnie Prince Charlie.

writing 'romances' was to make Scotland better known to the English, and to 'introduce her natives to those of the sister kingdom, in a more favourable light than they had been placed hitherto'. His first nine novels were set in his homeland, and include several of his finest books. If *Ivanhoe* is his masterpiece of pure storytelling, *The Heart of Midlothian, Old Mortality* and other tales of Scotland's turbulent history are more profound. They present moving conflicts based on fact, and the author's shifting sympathies reflect his special place at a crossroads in his country's evolution.

SCOTLAND'S HISTORY

In Scott's day, the country had become settled and 'civilized'. Edinburgh in particular – 'the Athens of the North' – boasted a society as cultured as any in Europe, and had produced such internationally renowned thinkers as the philosopher David Hume and the economist Adam Smith. Yet in 1745, only a generation before Scott's birth, wild Highlanders had risen for Bonnie Prince Charlie, occupied the Lowlands, and invaded England. Scott himself interviewed many of the survivors, and drew heavily on their memories. And, hardly further away in time, Royalist and robber, stern Covenanter and swaggering Jacobite had fashioned Scottish history into a pageant of wild passions and desperate loyalties.

As a man of the Enlightenment, Scott detested fanatics and upheld civilized order; but his imagination responded powerfully to the appeal of the old wild ways, and his novels pull our sympathies first one way, then

another. It is this tension between glamorous, ruinous romanticism and a saving but prosaic order that gives Scott's fiction much of its strength. The conflict exists between individuals, and even within individuals – in characters such as Edward Waverley, who begins as a soldier in the English army but then later transfers his allegiance to Bonnie Prince Charlie.

Scott realized his strengths and weaknesses as a novelist, and in a revealing passage in his *Journal* he compared himself, to his disadvantage, with Jane Austen: 'That young lady had a talent for describing the involvements and feelings and characters of ordinary life which is to me the most wonderful I ever met with. The Big Bow-wow strain I can do myself like any now going but the exquisite touch which renders ordinary common-place things and characters interesting from the truth of the description and the sentiment is denied to me.'

A BROAD VIEW

Scott's talents lay in quite another direction. He brought to history a new breadth of understanding, whose importance went far beyond the writing of fiction; and his influence on the European imagination would be very difficult to overrate. In purely literary terms he created the modern historical novel, which aims to 'get inside' a past age and see it in its own terms. In his own time he made the novel respectable and novel-writing a potentially well-paid if uncertain profession – achievements which make him the father-figure of Dickens, George Eliot and other literary giants of the 19th century.

Almost single-handed, Sir Walter Scott created the historical novel as we now know it. Summaries can never do full justice to the epic sweep of his books and the extraordinary variety of their vividly drawn characters. Beginning in 1814 with *Waverley*, which follows the fortunes of Bonnie Prince Charlie, Scott rapidly produced a series of novels based on the tumultuous history of 17th- and 18th-century Scotland, including *Old Mortality* (1816), *Rob Roy* (1817) and *The Heart of Midlothian* (1818), which is considered by some critics to be his finest novel. He then turned to the world of medieval English chivalry for his tenth novel, *Ivanhoe* (1819). His full range was subsequently revealed when he went on to write of Elizabethan England (*Kenilworth*, 1821), 15th-century France (*Quentin Durward*, 1823) and the Crusades (*The Talisman*, 1825). But, as *Redgauntlet* (1824) and *The Fair Maid of Perth* (1828) demonstrated, Scotland's history was never far from his thoughts. He was always inspired by his beloved country, and the tension between its romantic past and civilized present.

WAVERLEY
◆ 1814 ◆

A romantic young Englishman, Edward Waverley (left, in redcoats' uniform), the hero of Scott's first novel, becomes involved with the Jacobites, who supported the exiled Stuart kings and were most numerous in the Highlands of Scotland. Waverley joins the British army as an officer in 1745 and is sent to Scotland, where he meets a family friend, the Jacobite Bradwardine, and Bradwardine's gentle daughter Rose. Drawn to the Highlands by vague romantic feelings, Waverley encounters two ardent Jacobites, Fergus MacIvor and his beautiful sister Flora, with whom Waverley falls in love. These indiscreet contacts get him into serious trouble; accused of fomenting a mutiny, he is dismissed from the army in disgrace, and is saved from prison only with Rose's help. But Waverley passionately resents the way he has been treated, and his romantic interest in Jacobitism quickens into a dangerous commitment when Bonnie Prince Charlie, the son of the Stuart Pretender, lands in Scotland and raises his standard. Waverley fights for the Prince, whose cause is finally lost when his Highland troops are butchered at the Battle of Culloden. Waverley is lucky in securing a pardon, thanks to an influential officer whose life he has saved, and fate decides for him whether Flora or Rose shall be his bride.

Bendixen: Waverley/Fine Art Photographic Library

ROB ROY
◆ 1817 ◆

The famous outlaw Rob Roy Macgregor (right), a genuine historical character, gives his name to this novel, which takes place in 1715, at a time when the Jacobites – partisans of the exiled Stuart kings – were about to rise in arms (in *Waverley* Scott had already described the later, more famous rising under Bonnie Prince Charlie). Francis Osbaldistone, the son of a wealthy London merchant, refuses to join his father's business and is banished to his uncle's estate in the north of England. There he meets Diana Vernon, whose unmistakable preference for Francis arouses the jealous rage of his cousin, the scheming Rashleigh Osbaldistone. Rashleigh takes Francis's place in the counting house and sets out to destroy Francis and defraud the merchant. After various hazards, Francis makes a journey to the Highlands to enlist the help of Rob Roy, whose Jacobite sympathies have caused him to become an outlaw. In one of the big set-pieces of the novel, Francis witnesses an encounter between clansmen and redcoats from which Rob Roy makes one of his legendary escapes. With his assistance, Francis and Diana force Rashleigh to give up the money he has stolen, and when his further villainy is revealed – he is a traitor to the Jacobite cause – he has to face the wrath of Rob Roy Macgregor. When preparing for the novel, Scott visited Rob Roy's reputed cave, near Loch Lomond, and absorbed the local colour of Glasgow. His trouble was repaid, for the book was an instant success.

Kenneth Macleay: Rob Roy Macgregor. Asser Fine Arts, Chichester/Bridgeman Art Library

REDGAUNTLET
◆ 1824 ◆

The glamorous Bonnie Prince Charlie (above) features in *Redgauntlet*, in which Scott creates an imaginary episode of history – the Prince's secret return to Scotland several years after his defeat and flight in 1745. Two young friends, Darsie Latimer and Alan Fairford, unwittingly become involved in the evolving Jacobite plot. The romantic Darsie inherits some money and takes it into his head to visit the Border country. Meanwhile the more prosaic Alan is alarmed by two mysterious visitors who come to his law office. One is a Mr Herries, the other a beautiful lady in a green mantle who carries an urgent warning for Darsie. After various adventures, Darsie hears a supernatural story told by the blind fiddler, Wandering Willie, that highlights the diabolical reputation of the violently Jacobite Redgauntlet family. ('Wandering Willie's Tale', as it is known, has often been reprinted as a short story and is regarded as one of Scott's masterpieces in this field.) Then Darsie is kidnapped by Herries, actually Edward Redgauntlet, who is intent on using Darsie's influence on behalf of the Jacobite cause – for Darsie discovers to his astonishment that he himself is not only a Redgauntlet but the head of the entire family. However, Alan comes to the rescue, the friends foil Redgauntlet's schemes, and the Stuart cause is finally lost. Both young men are by now in love with 'Green Mantle', but the revelation of *her* identity leaves no doubt as to which of them she will choose. There are some intimate personal touches in *Redgauntlet*, not least of which is Scott's haunting memory of his first love, Williamina Belsches, whom he had in mind when he created Green Mantle.

THE HEART OF MIDLOTHIAN
◆ 1818 ◆

A riot in Edinburgh (right) – an event taken from history – provides the opening for this book, which is widely considered to be the finest of all the novels Scott wrote about his homeland. The Porteous riots of 1736 caused a sensation. Captain John Porteous, commander of Edinburgh's City Guard, had opened fire, without real justification, on a crowd assembled at an execution. Several members of the crowd were killed, and when it appeared that Porteous would escape punishment, a mob stormed Edinburgh's prison, the Tolbooth, nicknamed 'the Heart of Midlothian'. Porteous was dragged out and hanged. In Scott's version of the story, one of the mob's leaders is a wild young man, 'Robertson', actually the well-born George Staunton, who aims to exploit the situation in order to free the girl he loves, Effie Deans, who is incarcerated in the Tolbooth. But Effie, accused of child-murder, refuses to escape, since she hopes to prove her innocence. Her half-sister, Jeanie, is the true heroine of the book. She cannot bring herself to save Effie by giving false evidence, but when Effie is sentenced to death she sets out on foot for London. She arrives in time, secures an audience with Queen Caroline, and makes a moving appeal for her sister's life. Effie is pardoned and marries Staunton, but the supposedly murdered child comes back into their lives with ironic and fatal results. *The Heart of Midlothian* breaks new ground in its creation of a city's atmosphere and understanding of crowd psychology, features which were to remain unequalled until Dickens' early novels of the 1840s.

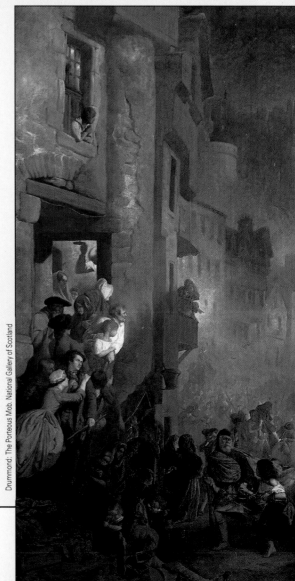

OLD MORTALITY
◆ 1816 ◆

The ruthless John Grahame of Claverhouse
(left), commander of Charles II's troops, sentences
to death Henry Morton, a brave and moderate
young man who has been caught up in a fanatical
religious struggle in 17th-century Scotland. The
title derives from a man nicknamed 'Old
Mortality', who repaired the tombs of
Covenanters – strict Presbyterians brutally
persecuted by the authorities. Morton escapes
death but endures exile, from which he returns to
reclaim his love, who is betrothed to a rival.

QUENTIN DURWARD
◆ 1823 ◆

**Quentin Durward, an adventurous young
Scot** (right), pauses at an inn with the Countess
Isabelle de Croye, a beautiful heiress whom he
protects and courts. In this tale of political
skulduggery and chivalric deeds set in 15th-century
France, Durward is a member of the bodyguard of
Louis XI of France, who is matched against his
presumptuous vassal, Charles the Bold, Duke of
Burgundy. The book's exciting climax decides the
fate not only of Durward and Isabelle, but also of
the French monarchy.

R. S. Lauder: Scene from Quentin Durward. Forbes Magazine Collection, New York/Bridgeman Art Library

KENILWORTH
◆ 1821 ◆

The romantic Kenilworth Castle (below) is
one of the settings for Scott's colourful pageant of
Elizabethan England, based on the real-life mystery
surrounding Amy Robsart. In the novel, Amy has
been persuaded to contract a secret marriage with
the Earl of Leicester in preference to her Cornish
suitor, Edmund Tressilian. But Leicester is afraid
of losing Queen Elizabeth's favour if his marriage
becomes known, so Amy is concealed at Cumnor
Place while Leicester receives a visit from Elizabeth
at Kenilworth. Amy is guarded by Richard
Varney, Leicester's trusted dependant, who
nevertheless hopes to make her his mistress.
Varney persuades Leicester that Amy and
Tressilian are lovers, and Leicester orders Varney
to avenge him by arranging an 'accident'. Leicester
eventually realizes his mistake, and Tressilian
rushes to Cumnor, hoping to save Amy's life.

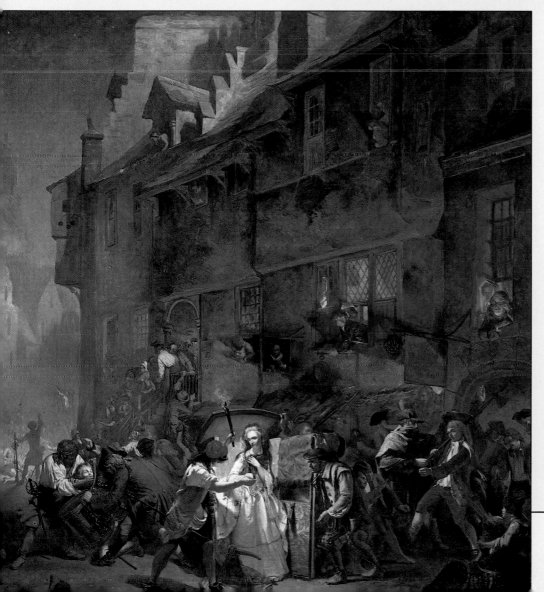

Victoria and Albert Museum/Bridgeman

The Age of Chivalry

Some of Scott's finest works were inspired by the romance of the Middle Ages, and were themselves a key factor in the 19th-century revival of chivalric ideals.

One of Sir Walter Scott's lesser known literary works is an article on chivalry he wrote for the *Encyclopaedia Britannica* in 1818, one year before the publication of *Ivanhoe*. He was regarded as an authority on the subject because of the vast store of antiquarian knowledge he had built up from studying the ancient ballads of Scotland. In his learned essay Scott described 'the total decay of the chivalrous principle' and tells how 'men learned to despise its fantastic refinements'; yet chivalry underwent a remarkable revival in Scott's lifetime, and he himself played a leading role in this.

Ivanhoe is set in the 1190s when chivalry was at its most active. The word was originally a collective term for knights or other mounted soldiers, then came to refer to the system of ethical values observed by this group. The Crusades (the series of wars undertaken by Christian nations of Europe against the Muslims) were chiefly responsible for the development of these ideals. Indeed, the first organized Orders of chivalry –

Courtly love
(below left) During the 12th century, poets in France developed a concept of courtly love that became an enduring theme in medieval literature. Central to it was the idea that the love of the knight for his lady should be a kind of ennobling religious devotion rather than a physical passion, and so convention established that she was in some way unattainable. In this exquisite 15th-century tapestry the lover offers his heart to his lady.

British Library/Michael Holford

Musée de Cluny, Paris/Bridgeman

dedicated to the care and protection of pilgrims to Jerusalem – were founded in the Holy Land in the early 12th century.

They were the Knights of the Order of the Hospital of St John of Jerusalem (Hospitallers) and the Poor Knights of Christ and of the Temple of Solomon (Templars). Both organizations became rich, international brotherhoods. The Templars, feared as a powerful secret society, were eventually suppressed by papal decree in 1312, and the Grand Master of the Order and several other members were burned at the stake as heretics. In *Ivanhoe*, the formidable Sir Brian de Bois-Guilbert is a Templar.

A knight owed loyalty to his spiritual master, God; to his temporal master, usually the king; and to the mistress of his heart, who in medieval literary romance was usually a woman married to someone else or otherwise unattainable (so that the love was 'pure'). But vital to the concept of chivalry was military glory. In *Ivanhoe*, when the hero is prevented by his wounds from taking part in the assault on Torquilstone Castle, he explains to his nurse Rebecca how he longs to be in the fray:

'*The love of the battle is the food upon which we live – the dust of the* mêlée *is the breath of our nostrils! We live not – we wish not to live – longer than while we are victorious and renowned – Such, maiden, are the laws of chivalry to which we are sworn, and to which we offer all that we hold dear.*'

The high-minded and kind-hearted Rebecca remonstrates with Ivanhoe: 'What remains to you as

The crusading spirit
(above) The Crusades were crucial to the development of chivalry, but the high ideals that led thousands of Christian soldiers to travel to the Holy Land to recapture Jerusalem from the Muslims all too easily degenerated into bloodlust. The First Crusade began in 1095, and Jerusalem was taken by siege (above) in 1099, after which the Crusaders carried out a horrible massacre of the Muslim and Jewish inhabitants. Jerusalem was recaptured by the Muslims in 1187, and Ivanhoe and Richard the Lionheart were part of the Third Crusade, which began in 1189 and failed to regain the Holy City.

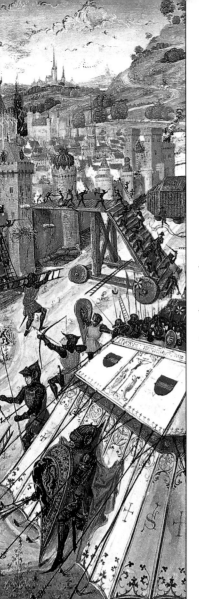

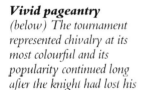

Lionhearted king
(right) Richard I, who throughout most of Ivanhoe is disguised as 'the Black Knight', represented the chivalric ideal of martial valour more completely than any other man of his day. He was an awesome warrior and his prowess made him a favourite topic for poets, as well as popular with his subjects. However, he was a failure as a king, with more interest in fighting than in governing his country. Here he is shown with his barons, but during his ten-year reign he spent no more than a few months in England.

the prize of all the blood you have spilled – of all the travail and pain you have endured – of all the tears which your deeds have caused, when death has broken the strong man's spear, and overtaken the speed of his war-horse?' Ivanhoe cries, 'Glory, maiden! Glory!'

Ivanhoe tells her, 'Thou art no Christian, Rebecca; and to thee are unknown those high feelings'. In so doing he reveals one of the great flaws in the chivalric ideal, for the fine sentiments to which a knight laid

claim extended only to those of his own class and beliefs. Rebecca is the noblest character in the novel, but because she is a Jewess she is treated with contempt. In practice, also, pious martial valour could descend into bloodlust, and refined courtly love into sordid adultery.

Although chivalry continued to be an enormously popular element in literature, in reality it was in decline by the 15th century. This was partly because the armoured horseman was no longer the dominant force on the battlefield. The English longbowmen who slaughtered the flower of French knighthood at the battles of Crecy (1346), Poitiers (1356) and Agincourt (1415) showed that war was now a matter of ruthless professionalism and technique.

CHIVALRY'S LONG SLUMBER
The pageantry of knighthood still continued on ceremonial occasions, however, and in the tournament – Henry VIII of England was a renowned combatant. In the reign of Elizabeth I there was an Indian summer of chivalry, centred on a cult of the Queen herself. One of Elizabeth's courtiers, the poet and soldier Sir Philip Sidney, was a real-life chivalric hero – renowned for his bravery and honour. As he lay fatally wounded on the battlefield of Zutphen in the Netherlands, he handed a proffered cup of water to an injured comrade with the words 'Thy necessity is yet greater than mine'. But in spite of such men, chivalry was by this time largely a matter of romantic nostalgia rather than a code for living. In the early years of the 17th century, Cervantes' immortal novel *Don Quixote* satirized the chivalric conventions as his ageing hero, whose mind has been unbalanced by reading too many chivalric romances, tilts at windmills and other imagined combatants.

Chivalry's long slumber lasted until the late 18th century, although elements of its code and trappings always survived – in heraldry, for example, and in certain traditions of manners and etiquette. The 18th century is known as the Age of Enlightenment, a time

Vivid pageantry
(below) The tournament represented chivalry at its most colourful and its popularity continued long after the knight had lost his

pre-eminence in battle. But in spite of the pageantry, the fighting was often grimly real and fatalities were common. In the tournament in Ivanhoe *four knights are killed and "upwards of thirty were desperately wounded".*

Fotomas

Renaissance chivalry
Soldier, statesman, poet, courtier and patron of the arts, Sir Philip Sidney was regarded as the ideal of chivalric courtesy. He died valiantly from battle wounds when he was only 31.

Regal rivalry
In 1520 Henry VIII of England and Francis I of France had a diplomatic meeting near Calais. The occasion was so splendid it was known as the Field of Cloth of Gold. Jousting was part of the lavish entertainment.

when civilized citizens strove to free themselves from superstition and championed the cause of human reason. In such an intellectual climate the ideals of chivalry seemed ridiculous rather than noble, and in his *History of Great Britain*, David Hume, one of the leading philosophers of the Enlightenment, called the Crusades 'the most signal and durable monument of human folly that has yet appeared in any age or nation'.

Paradoxically, however, the rational spirit that guided Hume helped to create a new interest in all aspects of medieval life, including chivalry. Historians of the time approached the past in a new, objective fashion, and began to study medieval documents and artifacts with scientific curiosity. Whereas the rationalists of the Enlightenment showed a scholarly attitude to the distant past, it was the very distance and mystery of the Middle Ages which appealed to the Romantics of the late 18th and early 19th century.

Since chivalry appealed to the emotions rather than the intellect, it stirred the imagination of Romantic poets. Scott was too level-headed to be called a true Romantic, but he was so deeply steeped in the literature and history of the Middle Ages that he handled medieval subjects with effortless flair.

About a third of Scott's novels are devoted to medieval themes. Apart from *Ivanhoe*, the best known are *Quentin Durward* and *The Talisman*; and the narrative poems which made him famous are very much concerned with chivalry and romance. Both poems and novels reached an astonishingly wide audience – and not just in Britain. In 1811, for example, Louis Simond, a French traveller visiting England, compared Windsor Castle to 'a castle of Sir Walter Scott's own building'. And Sir Adam Ferguson read aloud a stirring battle description from Scott's *The Lady of the Lake* to encourage his troops when they were under attack during the war against Napoleon in Portugal. *Ivanhoe* achieved unprecedented heights of popularity, for in

the year after it was published no fewer than five dramatized versions of the chivalric tale were being shown in London.

Scott's influence can also be seen in the visual arts of the time. After the success of *Ivanhoe*, it was unusual for the Royal Academy summer exhibition not to include at least one picture illustrating a scene from the book; and Scott's house at Abbotsford initiated the style called Scots Baronial that became all the rage in mid-19th century Scotland. Scott wanted his house to be like an 'old English hall such as a squire of yore dwelt in'.

DAZZLING PAGEANTRY

The revival of the chivalrous spirit manifested itself most clearly and colourfully, however, in the field of pageantry. From the early years of the 19th century, the monarchy seized on every opportunity to dress up the Court in the most magnificent anachronistic fashion. One instance was the great installation ceremony for Knights of the Garter held at Windsor Castle on St George's day in 1805. The breathtaking ceremonial was followed by superb banquets, and a contemporary chronicler wrote, 'It was his majesty's [George III's] particular wish, that as many of the old customs should be kept up as possible.' At a time when Britain was locked in a mighty struggle with Napoleon (this was the year of the Battle of Trafalgar) it made sound sense, as the chronicler put it, 'to cherish that chivalrous spirit . . . which burned in the breasts of our ancestors' and 'to fan the flame of loyalty and patriotism'.

The pomp and magnificence was even greater at George IV's coronation in 1821. Scott was a guest at the ceremony, and said that foreign dignitaries present were 'utterly astonished and delighted to see the revival of feudal dresses and feudal grandeur when the occasion demanded it, and that in a degree of splendour which, they averred, they had never seen paralleled in Europe'. The following year, the new King George visited Edin-

burgh, and Scott was chosen to direct the pageantry that accompanied his regal progress.

When Queen Victoria was crowned in 1838, however, pageantry was severely curtailed. The Prime Minister, Lord Melbourne, thought conspicuous display would be inappropriate at a time of economic depression. Melbourne was a Whig (a member of the party that favoured political and social reform) and his Tory opponents were outraged by the 'Penny Coronation', which they felt was an attack on the monarchy, not just on tradition.

This feeling led to the most famous and most farcical display of chivalric revival – the Eglinton Tournament. Lord Eglinton, a rich young Tory, decided to hold a tournament to flaunt the values that had been spurned by the Government. The tournament was arranged for 28 August 1839 at Eglinton Castle in Scotland, and the interest it aroused was enormous, requests for tickets even coming from India and South America.

Scott's account of the tournament in *Ivanhoe* was a major source of inspiration to Lord Eglinton. A huge amount of preparation was involved in organizing the

The Black Prince wins his spurs

(above) At the Battle of Crécy in 1346 Edward III's son, Edward the Black Prince, then only 16, conducted himself with conspicuous gallantry. He was one of the original Knights of the Garter, a British Order of chivalry.

The tournament revived

(right) The Eglinton Tournament of 1839 was the most spectacular event in the Victorian revival of chivalry, but it was ruined by the rain. One participant said he had never seen 'the disagreeable and the ridiculous so completely mixed together'. Another said 'the rain began, and the knights threw down their lances, and put up their umbrellas.' When the weather cleared they salvaged some pride and jousted successfully.

Medieval inspiration
(above) Many 19th-century artists were
inspired by chivalric romance. This tapestry
designed by Sir Edward Burne-Jones shows
an episode from Arthurian legend.

Nostalgic fancy dress
(below) In 1842 Queen Victoria gave a
costume ball at Buckingham Palace. Most
guests wore medieval costume and some
dressed as characters from Scott's novels.

armour (most of it hired from a London dealer), cos-
tumes and marquees, and in practising the lost art of
jousting. It proved particularly difficult for the young
noblemen taking part in the tournament to persuade
their horses to gallop close enough to the barrier that
separated the charging knights, but a dress rehearsal
went off very well.

When the great day arrived, spirits were high and the
audience 100,000 strong. The tournament opened with
a procession, but just as it got under way a clap of thun-
der announced a torrential rainstorm that lasted
throughout the day. Soon participants and spectators
were drenched, the horses slithered in the mud, and the
whole affair degenerated into a fiasco. However, Lord
Eglinton refused to be downcast, and when the weather cheered up a couple of days later, he arranged
jousting and banqueting with some success. But it was
the farcical element that was to be remembered. Whig
newspapers had a field day, and a knight with an
umbrella came to symbolize the tournament.

Despite the ludicrous aspects of the Eglinton Tournament, the chivalric ideal became part of Victorian
culture. Victoria's consort, Prince Albert, seemed to
the Queen to be the embodiment of knightly virtue and
she loved to see him in armour. In 1842 she held a lavish
costume ball in which she and her husband went
dressed as Edward III and his wife Queen Philippa.
This delight in medieval trappings also featured in a
revival of interest in Arthurian legend which affected
both literature and art (for example, the poems of
Alfred, Lord Tennyson and the paintings of the Pre-
Raphaelites).

A 'GENTLEMANLY' IDEAL

The chivalric ideal also coloured the whole notion of
what it was to be a 'gentleman' – someone who was
loyal to Queen and country, who treated women with
reverence, who preferred death to dishonour and stood
up for truth and fair play. It was an ideal which charac-
terized such men as Sir Arthur Conan Doyle – whose
preoccupations with honour and patriotism imbued his
literature, and his life in the army and on the cricket-
field. Indeed, sport was seen almost entirely in chivalric terms, and the popular magazine *Punch* described
the qualities of a good sportsman thus:

'He is one who has not merely braced his muscles
and developed his endurance by the exercise of some
great sport, but has . . . learnt to control his anger, to be
considerate to his fellow men . . . to bear aloft a cheer-
ful countenance under disappointment, and never own
himself defeated until the last breath is out of his body.'

These ideals continued into the 20th century – Sir
Robert Baden-Powell's *Scouting for Boys*, published in
1908, the year in which he founded the Boy Scouts
movement, is full of chivalric imagery. Significantly,
Ivanhoe was one of the books he recommended scouts
to read. It was World War I that sounded the death
knell of chivalry. St George figured prominently in
wartime propaganda, but after millions had been
slaughtered it was impossible to pretend that war was
a glorious adventure. As Scott put it in his essay on
chivalry, 'We can now only look back on it as a beautiful and fantastic piece of frostwork, which has dissolved
in the beams of the sun!'

ROBERT LOUIS STEVENSON

→ *1850-1894* →

Robert Louis Stevenson was one of the greatest of all adventure
writers. Few have rivalled his gift for telling a rattling yarn, but
he also had a powerful moral sense and an acute psychological
perception. His own short life was packed with incident, travel
and adventure, and was strongly motivated by his belief that
'no man is of any use until he has dared everything'. Handsome,
witty, generous to a fault, but living always in the shadow of
ill health, he was a truly Romantic figure.

Fragile Adventurer

Undeterred by his physical frailty, Robert Louis Stevenson travelled half-way round the world in pursuit of a dream – he wanted love and adventure, and found them both.

Tall and attractive, with bewitching eyes, Robert Louis Stevenson was a man who made friends easily. Whimsical by nature and outlandish in attire, he never fitted comfortably in the genteel ambience of his birth and from his earliest days was filled with a longing to travel. 'You must understand,' he once wrote to his mother, 'that I shall be a nomad, more or less, until my days be done.'

Stevenson was born on 13 November 1850 in Edinburgh. His father, Thomas, came from the great lighthouse engineering family. His mother Margaret, known as Maggie – with whom Stevenson shared a lung weakness that brought him close to death on many occasions – was the daughter of a clergyman. A wife and mother at barely 20, she was a light-hearted, optimistic woman. But Thomas Stevenson's background of covenanting Presbyterianism left him prey to brooding fits of despair. Nevertheless, he was a kind man, with a soft spot for stray dogs, and in their house at Howard Place he and Maggie doted on their first and only child.

A sick-room atmosphere prevailed in the household. Stevenson's mother was a semi-invalid who was often confined to bed, and Stevenson himself was a sickly, puny child, prone to nightmares. He was affectionately known as 'Smout', a Scots colloquialism meaning 'small fry'. In his early years he saw more of his nurse Alison Cunningham than he did of his mother.

Portrait by G. Fiddes Watt. City of Edinburgh Museums & Art Galleries

Adoring parents

Youthful and vivacious, Maggie Stevenson doted on her 'wean' (standing by her, right) – and he on her. So struck was she by his precocity that she recorded all his first utterances in an almanack and continued to keep a diary of his sayings throughout his life. Her husband, Thomas Stevenson (inset right), was ten years her senior. A lighthouse engineer and notable inventor, he blended, according to his son's later recollections, 'sterness and softness' in a manner 'that was wholly Scottish'.

Key Dates

1850 born in Edinburgh

1867 enters Edinburgh University

1871 takes up law

1875 meets W. E. Henley

1876 meets Fanny Van de Grift Osbourne

1879 sails for America

1880 marries Fanny

1883 *Treasure Island*

1885 settles in Bournemouth; *A Child's Garden of Verses*

1886 *Dr Jekyll and Mr Hyde* and *Kidnapped*

1888 sails to South Seas

1889 buys Vailima estate in Samoa

1894 dies at Vailima

Beloved Nanny

Alison Cunningham (above right), known as 'Cummie', was Louis' second mother. It was she who sat by his bed through his long nights of sickness, and she to whom he dedicated A Child's Garden of Verses.

Edinburgh's splendours

Stevenson grew up in the genteel elegance of Edinburgh's more affluent city streets, surrounded by the Georgian legacy of crescents, rows of terraces and large, open squares. Although he was to seek out the low life of the city and feel more at home in the 'beggarly slums', this was not what he was born to and was a source of much concern to his parents.

SKELT'S NEW SMUGGLERS

Pubd by E. SKELT.   Nº 2

Playroom adventures

Armed with a toy theatre and sets of exciting characters, the young Louis practised his gifts for storytelling.

'Cummie' was a morbidly religious woman who read nothing but devout tracts to her young charge, implanting many 'ecstasies and terrors' in his fevered imagination. His favourite game at this time was 'playing at church', making a pulpit of a chair and sermonizing from it. 'I piped and snivelled over the Bible', he remarked in later life.

The family moved from Howard Place, first to Inverleith Terrace – where Stevenson fell ill with the croup and bronchitis – then, when he was six, to the splendid New Town terrace of Heriot Row. It was on the third floor of this house that he played with the swashbuckling cardboard cut-out figures from the toy theatres called *Skelt's Juvenile Dramas*. This developed the taste for the sort of adventure that was to loom so large in both his tales and his adult life. His enthusiastic playmate then, as in years to come, was his dreamy cousin Bob.

Stevenson attended a local school when he was seven, followed by the Edinburgh Academy. Later, while his mother wintered abroad for her health, he went to a boarding school in Surrey, which he hated. Thomas Stevenson's ambition for his son – that he should enter the family lighthouse business – seemed firmly on course. At 17, he was sent to inspect the harbour works of Fife and Caithness, and in 1867 he entered Edinburgh University to study engineering.

On his own admission Stevenson was an idle student. His 'own private end' at this time was to learn

The handwritten letter shows text including near bottom "Birds chirrup, Crickets cri,"

Literary connections
Six years Louis' senior, Sidney Colvin (above) helped launch Louis into London's literary society. The two had met through Mrs Frances Sitwell, a beautiful and brilliant woman whom Louis revered and called his 'Madonna' (line 3 of letter, above), and whom Colvin also loved. Although she was to marry Colvin, the three remained lifelong friends.

how to become a writer. In his famous phrase he played 'the sedulous ape' to such models as Charles Lamb, William Wordsworth and Daniel Defoe, imitating their work and reading widely. And in 1871 he announced to his long-suffering father that his chosen career was not to be lighthouse engineering, but writing. Thomas Stevenson took this news calmly enough, believing it to be no more than a youthful fad. He merely stipulated that Stevenson should study law to provide a steady occupation should the writing fail.

Stevenson's youthful rebellion against the strict Presbyterian conformity of his childhood reached a peak at this time. With his incorrigible cousin Bob he haunted the brothels of Edinburgh and the port of Leith, and smoked hashish in the lowest taverns, 'the companion of seamen, chimney sweeps and thieves', who called him 'Velvet Coat' because of the bohemian jacket he always wore.

'MADMAN OR FOOL'
In 1873 the aspiring young writer dropped a bombshell that precipitated a crisis in the family. He told Thomas Stevenson he was a non-believer. To his father this was simply not a credible point of view – only a 'madman or a fool' could fail to believe in God. Stevenson's admission poisoned the atmosphere at Heriot Row. It was, he said, 'like a house in which somebody is still waiting burial'. His parents paced about with long faces, and stormy arguments were followed by periods of grim silence.

Finally his parents attempted to cure their son once and for all of his heretical nonsense and packed him off

to stay with his cousin Maud, who had married a sensible English clergyman. His stay at Cockfield Rectory near Bury St Edmunds did not have the desired effect, however. Instead, he fell headlong and hopelessly in love with a house guest.

Frances Sitwell – 'Madonna', as he came to call her – was, at 34, 12 years his senior, and the separated wife of a clergyman who had had a not entirely professional interest in choirboys. In no time Stevenson was pour-

Artist friend
John Singer Sargent was a friend of the Stevensons, and a frequent visitor to their house in Bournemouth. He painted them there with Fanny resplendent in Indian garb, and Louis in his familiar velvet jacket.

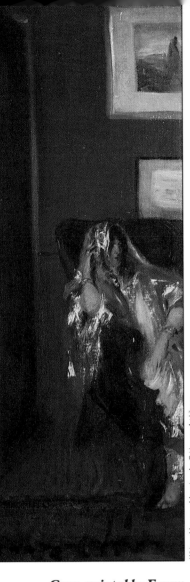

ing his heart out to 'Madonna' on long country walks. Mrs Sitwell coped gracefully with his youthful ardour. She certainly did not reciprocate his passion, but Stevenson did impress her as a precocious literary talent, and it was through her that he struck up a most fruitful, lasting friendship with the distinguished Cambridge academic Sidney Colvin.

Colvin introduced Stevenson to the refined literary air of the Savile Club in London, and helped set him on a fledgling writing career as a contributor to magazines while he continued to study at the Scottish Bar. At this time too Stevenson met the invalid poet W. E. Henley, with whom he had a turbulent friendship that was to end in mutual bitterness.

For some years, plagued by ill health, Stevenson journeyed restlessly around Scotland and England as well as France, joking in a letter to his mother that she had a tramp and a vagabond for a son. Time had not, however, lessened his determination to be a writer, much to his father's regret. Despite passing his law exams and ceremoniously fixing a brass advocate's plate to the door of number 17 Heriot Row, Stevenson never practised at the Bar. Instead he was soon back in France mixing with the company he liked best – carefree bohemians. When he returned to Edinburgh in the autumn of 1875 he fell into a fit of black depression. He was not to know that on the other side of the bleak Scottish winter waited the fulcrum and love of his life.

A MOMENTOUS MEETING

Stevenson and his cousin Bob had spent a number of summers at Grez, an artists' colony on the edge of the Fontainebleau forest, 60 miles from Paris. Before their next visit word reached them of a stunning addition to the bohemian enclave, a beautiful American woman and her 'bewitching' daughter and son.

Fanny Van de Grift Osbourne had withdrawn to the hotel at Grez after the death of her youngest son in Paris. Her estranged husband had returned to America shortly afterwards. There was much talk of what the 'mad Stevensons' would make of her. Bob Stevenson,

the artist and rake, was first on the scene - and he stole her heart. She described him as 'the most beautiful creature I ever saw in my life'. But she had reckoned without Louis (as Robert Louis was known).

Louis Stevenson literally vaulted into Fanny's life in early July 1876. The hotel guests were seated at dinner, with Fanny and her daughter Belle the inevitable centre of chivalrous attention, when there was a noise outside the open window and a shabby figure wearing a hat and carrying a knapsack jumped lightly into the room. 'My cousin Louis Stevenson', announced Bob suavely, like a conjuror. Belle was to claim later that it was love at first sight between the 25-year old Stevenson and her mother.

Over the next two years their love affair deepened and in 1878 Stevenson took his father into his confidence and declared his intention of marrying this woman, who was ten years his senior, still married, and had two children to support. With a resignation that came more easily to him by this time, Thomas Stevenson hardly batted an eyelid – this was just another of his son's whimsical schemes.

Indeed, it seemed to be the case when Fanny and her children abruptly returned to San Francisco. Desolate and confused, Stevenson went to France on his own, hired a donkey called Modestine and tramped around the mountainous countryside of the Cévennes. He could not, however, stop thinking about Fanny.

Back in London and Edinburgh, Stevenson – now a regular magazine contributor – remained gloomy and sickly. His love for Fanny never wavered and he immediately responded to a distraught telegram from her in Monterey, California. He bought a steamship ticket, and, without telling his parents (and against the advice of his literary friends), he set sail from Greenock on 7 August 1879 aboard the SS *Devonia*, bound for New York on the first lap of his journey to California.

The story of his sea voyage and his nightmarish trip West aboard emigrant trains is told in *The Amateur Emigrant*, a tribute to his determination to write and record even amid the most appalling squalor and

Grez, painted by Fanny (below) *By chance, Fanny Osbourne chose to retreat to the French artists' colony at Grez after the death of her youngest son. It was there, in the summer of 1876, that she met the 25-year-old Louis.*

TIGER AND TIGER LILY

Born in Indiana in 1840, Fanny Van de Grift was married at 17 and had three children before she finally left her philandering husband. In the intervening years she had followed him to the most primitive, lawless silver-mining towns of Nevada, had for a time believed him dead (killed by Indians), and had started a new life for herself in San Franscisco.

Unconventional and spirited, she moved with her children to Europe where she met Stevenson (right), who called her his 'tiger and tiger lily'.

City of Edinburgh Museums & Art Galleries

BBC Hulton Picture Library

Fact or Fiction

WILLIAM ERNEST HENLEY

Stevenson based the turncoat rogue, Long John Silver, on his poet friend and literary collaborator W. E. Henley. Henley, with his bushy hair and red beard was a noisy, argumentative man who enjoyed his whisky. As a boy he had had a foot amputated and Stevenson once wrote to him, 'It was the sight of your maimed strength and masterfulness that begot John Silver.'

BBC Hulton Picture Library

despite his own deteriorating health. Nearly dead on his feet, he finally made it to Monterey and his lover's side.

After tribulations of ill health and poverty, the fairy story of Stevenson's love for Fanny had its happy resolution when they were married in San Francisco on 19 May 1880. Their honeymoon was also of a fairy tale quality: a two-month sojourn in an abandoned silver-mining shack on Mount St Helena in the Napa Valley, which Stevenson recaptured in the pages of *The Silverado Squatters*.

The newly-weds returned to Europe, and were reconciled with Stevenson's parents. The new Stevenson family, including Fanny's son Lloyd, now lived in Scotland and spent two winters at the health resort of Davos in the Swiss Alps. During this time Stevenson wrote the book that would ensure his literary fame – the adventure classic *Treasure Island*. He wrote it as much for his father as for his cherished stepson Lloyd. For the book, to his joy and amazement, he was offered 'A hundred jingling, tingling, golden-minted quid'!

After spells in the Highlands and the south of France the Stevensons settled in Bournemouth, where the frail

writer was later to liken his life to that of 'a pallid weevil in a biscuit'. Nevertheless, he now entered a most productive phase of his writing career, completing *A Child's Garden of Verses, Kidnapped,* and that Gothic shocker, *The Strange Case of Dr Jekyll and Mr Hyde.* And it was at Bournemouth that Stevenson formed a lasting and mutually admiring friendship with the great American novelist, Henry James.

SOUTH SEAS ADVENTURE

Following the death of his father in May 1887, Stevenson, his mother, Fanny and Lloyd set sail for America on an odyssey that would take them half-way round the world. Now a celebrated writer, Stevenson was abashed by the attention he received in New York. The family settled first at Saranac Lake in the Adirondack Mountains where, as the temperature dropped to 40° below zero, Stevenson put to one side the book he was working on – *The Master of Ballantrae* – and set about turning a long cherished dream into reality; he would hire a boat and venture into the mysterious world of the South Seas.

Samoan sanctuary
When completed, Vailima, painted (top) by Belle, Stevenson's step-daughter, boasted a 50-foot main hall with marble busts and originals by Rodin and Piranesi. Here Stevenson, with his family, spent the happiest days of his life. In the photo Lloyd is standing between Stevenson and his redoubtable mother, with Belle and her son below Fanny. Of her mother-in-law Fanny wrote to Henry James, 'I wish you could but just get a glimpse of that lady taking a moonlight promenade on the beach in the company of a gentleman dressed in a single handkerchief.'

City of Edinburgh Museums & Art Galleries

'Ea Haere ia Oe' by P. Gauguin. Hermitage, Leningrad/Bridgeman Art Library

That boat was the schooner *Casco,* which slid out from San Francisco Bay at the end of June 1888 and took the Stevensons to the Marquesas Islands, Tahiti and Honolulu. Stevenson's friends back home – with the honourable exception of Henry James – never really forgave him his self-imposed exile. The fact was he had 'more fun and pleasure of my life these past months than ever before, and more health than any time in ten long years.'

SETTLING DOWN

After more island adventuring and further health crises Stevenson found his final home in December 1889 – at Apia, the capital of Upolu in the Samoan Islands. Here, in several hundred acres of ground, he built a magnificent wooden house called Vailima, filled it with elegant furniture from the family home in far-away Heriot Row, assembled round him a loyal house-hold of Samoan servants, and installed himself, Fanny and her children, and his elderly, redoubtable mother Maggie. And now, amid this subtropical lushness, his thoughts turned to the homeland he would never again

Polynesian paradise
Like Gauguin, a few years later, Stevenson fell in love with Tahiti (above), enchanted by the lushness of the land and the friendliness of the people.

Final days
(Top left) One of many photographs of Stevenson and family in Samoa shows the novelist playing his flageolet in bed at Vailima. When he died, 40 chieftains chopped and axed a path up the steep face of Mount Vaea for Stevenson's grave (above left), knowing that this was the resting place that their cherished storyteller had wanted.

set eyes on, and he *"heard again/In my precipitous city beaten bells/Winnow the keen sea wind. And here afar,/ Intent on my own race and place, I wrote . . ."*

The writing in question was *Weir of Hermiston,* an unfinished fragment generally regarded as a master-piece. Stevenson had been working on this when, on 3 December 1894, he wandered out on to the verandah to talk to Fanny. Suddenly he held his hands to his head, cried out, 'What's that? Do I look strange?', and col-lapsed on the floor. He never regained consciousness.

Ironically, after the courageous lifelong battle he had fought against his treacherous lung disease, Robert Louis Stevenson died of a brain haemorrhage. He was aged 44, had never been fitter and was on the point of gaining full maturity as a writer.

In accordance with his wishes he was buried on the summit of Mount Vaea. His coffin was draped with the red ensign from the *Casco.* The bronze plaque on his tomb bears these famous lines from his poem *Requiem:*

> *Here he lies where he longed to be;*
> *Home is the sailor home from the sea,*
> *And the hunter home from the hill.*

Map — Mansell Collection

59

TREASURE ISLAND

Allowing the *Hispaniola's* band of brigands free rein, Stevenson creates an adventure classic packed with skulduggery, murder and betrayal.

Swashbuckling, pig-tailed pirates; a voyage to a remote island; a map of buried treasure; sea-shanties with an ominous reminder of death and destruction – these are just some of the elements which make *Treasure Island* a classic adventure story, and have kept it a favourite for more than a hundred years.

It was conceived by Robert Louis Stevenson as 'a story for boys . . . Women were excluded'. But *Treasure Island* has an appeal for both sexes and all ages, with its action-packed narrative and its convincing and often fearsome characters.

Treasure Island was Stevenson's first full-length work of fiction. It is a short novel whose excitement and atmosphere can best be savoured by reading it aloud (as Stevenson did during its creation) or by reading it at a single uninterrupted sitting (as the statesman William Gladstone is reported to have done when it was first published).

GUIDE TO THE PLOT

Set in the 18th century, the story opens in a remote part of south-west England where its narrator and hero, Jim Hawkins, a teenage boy, is helping his mother and sickly father to run their inn, The Admiral Benbow. Into this lonely, uneventful setting comes Captain Billy Bones, with his "black broken nails", his "bad clothes", his coarse way of speaking, his desire to remain hidden from any passing sea-faring men, and his habit, when he has taken too much rum, of terrorizing the company of the inn with his stories "about hanging, and walking the plank, and storms at sea".

One day, Black Dog, "a pale tallowy creature, wanting two fingers of the left hand", comes looking for the captain. There is a quarrel and a fight. Black Dog takes to his heels, and the captain, who had looked "old and sick" at his appearance, suffers a stroke.

A few days later, a blind beggar, a dreadful-looking figure with a cruel, cold and ugly

The Admiral Benbow
Captain Billy Bones' quiet stay at the Inn is broken by the untimely arrival of Black Dog (right).

Trampled to death
(right) Pursued by men on horseback, the villainous buccaneers disperse and make a run for it, but Blind Pew is left behind to fend for himself. Unable to gauge where the noise is coming from, he bolts into a ditch and then, picking himself up, dashes straight under the hooves of an advancing horse: "Pew was dead, stone dead."

E.T. Archive

Mutiny on deck
(above and left) The voyage of the Hispaniola is ill-fated from the start. The crew are a mutinous bunch, as Captain Smollett had suspected, and it is only a matter of time before Long John Silver's promises and the thought of all that treasure cause their allegiances to shift and fights to break out on deck.

eventfully. But when the ship approaches the island, Jim overhears a conversation which confirms Captain Smollett's worst fears – a mutiny is at hand. The pirates want to keep the treasure for themselves and Silver 'claims' Trelawney – "I'll wring his calf's head off his body with these hands." Jim tells his trusted friends, the doctor, the captain and the squire, what he has heard.

A number of the pirates go ashore while others guard the ship, and Jim sets off immediately on his own explorations. Dr Livesey also goes ashore and discovers the stockade, a ready-made place from which to attack, and defend themselves against the enemy. The squire's party duly establish

voice also comes in search of the captain. The blind man delivers the "black spot" – a deadly summons – and Captain Bill promptly dies.

Jim and his mother search the captain's sea-chest for money to settle his debts. In addition to some of the money owed to them, Jim removes an oilskin package from the chest, just managing to escape the return of the blind man and his fellow buccaneers.

A rescue party takes Jim to deliver the oilskin package into the safekeeping of Dr Livesey. The doctor is dining with Squire Trelawney who becomes very excited at the possibility that the package might reveal the whereabouts of the renowned Captain Flint's treasure. The package indeed contains such a map and the squire is anxious to equip a ship and set off at once in pursuit of the treasure.

But the squire, though amiable, is neither shrewd nor discreet. He enlists a crew, partly from his own faithful retainers, but largely from those recommended by Long John Silver, a one-legged former seaman whom he meets 'by chance' in Bristol. Jim is invited to join them.

The newly appointed Captain Smollett voices his disquiet about the trip and the crew of the *Hispaniola*, but the squire dismisses his fears as unfounded.

The outward journey passes relatively un-

Quayside walk
Jim is transfixed by his "most interesting" companion who regales him with nautical tales.

> "Now, look you here, Jim Hawkins," he said, in a steady whisper, that was no more than audible "you're within half a plank of death, and, what's a long sight worse, of torture."

themselves there. Later, Jim joins them with news of a half-demented stranger he has encountered, Ben Gunn, a member of Flint's original crew, who has been marooned on the island for three long years, surviving on "goats . . . and berries and oysters".

The following day an attack is launched on the stockade. Captain Smollett is injured but greater damage is inflicted on the pirates. The doctor sets off to consult with Ben Gunn, while Jim finds Gunn's roughly made boat and embarks on a perilous attempt to cut loose the *Hispaniola*, now sporting "the Jolly Roger, the black flag of piracy". He boards the ship and finds that the mutinous crew have turned against each other, with Israel Hands being the only survivor. Together they direct the ship to a suitable beaching point, but Hands suddenly attacks Jim and all seems to be lost .

Living dangerously
(right) To Silver, common pirates are much-revered "gentlemen of fortune". "They lives rough, and they risk swinging, but they eat and drink like fighting-cocks."

Fight to the death
(left) Caught in mortal combat with Israel Hands, Jim suddenly gains an advantage: "One more step . . . and I'll blow your brains out."

The dead buccaneer
Intent on tracking down the treasure, the pirates stumble on a human skeleton and are filled with terror. "Tain't in natur", one exclaims, seeing the bizarre way that the body lies.

After some exciting turns of event, Jim manages to reach the shore and make his way back to the stockade which he finds, to his dismay, has been taken over by the pirates, who have also gained possession of the treasure map. They seize Jim, and Silver whispers to him, "you're within half a plank of death, and, what's a long sight worse, of torture." But Silver feels his position is somewhat precarious. He begins playing his usual tricky game of keeping his options open with both sides. If he can get to the treasure and keep it he will; if not, he hopes to achieve some credit with the doctor to ensure more lenient treatment back in England.

With Jim tied to him by a rope, Silver and the remaining five pirates start in search of the treasure. Spooked by deathly sounds and apparitions along the way, they panic – "the colour went from their six faces like enchantment; some leaped to their feet, some clawed hold of others." Eventually, spurred on by Silver, they reach the spot, and thinking of the 700,000 pounds of gold "their eyes burned in their heads". But they are too late – the treasure is gone. The five villains turn on Silver, but they in turn are attacked by the doctor, Gray, the carpenter's mate, and Ben Gunn who emerge from the trees. A bloody fight ensues and allegiances shift. Finally, the secret of the missing treasure is revealed, the "treasure that we had come so far to seek, and that

had cost already the lives of seventeen men from the *Hispaniola*." Into whose hands it finally falls, and just what happens to Long John Silver, remains to be seen . . .

A ROMANTIC ADVENTURE

Treasure Island is an adventure story written principally for young people, boys in particular. But it touches the romantic and childish elements in adults too – so that it has been reliably reported that 'elderly men have gulped [it] down unashamed to have become boys for a spell'.

Stevenson believed that the creative writer had a duty to satisfy the 'nameless longings of the reader and to obey the ideal laws of the daydream'. Jim Hawkins' adventures do just that. An unremarkable young boy leading an uneventful life is suddenly removed to an exotic location and is given repeated opportunities to become a hero.

First he secures the map, then he discovers the pirates' plot. Next he meets and enlists the co-operation of Ben Gunn, who is vital to the successful outcome of the story. He goes on to

> *"The thought of the money, as they drew nearer, swallowed up their previous terrors. Their eyes burned in their heads; their feet grew speedier and lighter; their whole soul was bound up in that fortune, that whole lifetime of extravagance and pleasure, that lay waiting there for each of them."*

rescue a ship from pirates, declare himself master of it and outwit a wily old pirate several times his age. Who could dream of more?

Yet *Treasure Island* is a tale grounded in reality. Both the plot and the characterization are constructed with concrete details which are both credible and compelling. The reader is exasperated by Squire Trelawney's impulsiveness and lack of judgement. For example, it is entirely consistent with the squire's character that he should be taken in by Long John Silver, and dismiss the good advice of Captain Smollett. Once he has done this, the plot moves forward inexorably. The voyage goes ahead with its scheming crew, and danger erupts, as it must, when the squire and his party are far from help and home.

Treasure Island is a story vividly and dramatically told. Stevenson said that he visualized his novels in a 'series of small, bright, restless pictures'. The inventive force behind it, and the vividness of its narrative, have made it popular with a wide audience. But it is also much more than just a rattling good tale. The story is told with a light touch that also has a darker side, and it is this darker side that makes its outcome more subtle and so more satisfying.

LIGHT AND DARK

We can see in the character of Jim Hawkins the effect of the treasure hunt. At the outset he is full of romantic notions of adventure and excitement: "full of sea-dreams and the most charming anticipations of strange islands and adventures." By the time he returns, he seems older and wiser. He knows now that people are not always what they seem – having taken Silver into his trust and his affections, he finally discovers him to be a "prodigious villain and impostor". He appreciates also the price of adventure: "How many it [the treasure] had cost in the amassing, what blood and sorrow, what good ships scuttled on the deep, what brave men walking the plank blindfold, what shot of cannon, what shame and lies and cruelty, perhaps no man alive could tell." Though there is more treasure and more adventures to be had, Jim wants nothing more to do with it.

The seriousness of the situation was apparent from the outset, in the fear and isolation in which Captain Bill lived; and in the ominous message of the sea-shanty he sang: "*Fifteen men on The Dead Man's Chest –*". The island itself is rank, harbours disease and disgorges unpleasant vapours at night – a far cry from the wondrous place of Jim's imaginings.

Chris Collingwood

Gaining the treasure
With the gold between his fingers, Jim is suddenly appalled. "How many it had cost in the amassing, what blood and sorrow . . . what shame and lies and cruelty, perhaps no man alive could tell."

Stevenson has been accredited with (or accused of) an 'uncanny coalition with villainy'. In other words he seemed attracted by the dark and villainous aspects of human nature, and could identify with, and give flesh to, evil characters just as readily as virtuous ones. The power of Long John Silver's character is such that he creates a dilemma in our minds – we cannot entirely like him, because he is 'bad', but on the other hand we cannot wholly dislike him because he is clever and beguiling.

Stevenson was definitely somewhat enamoured of his own creation, and it is no coincidence that of all the pirates, Silver is the only one to survive and escape with some chance of success. It seems somehow fitting that such a character should be left at large, roaming the seas, ready to leap into another childlike imagination just as the crew of the *Hispaniola* leapt into Stevenson's.

| In the Background |

RULES OF PIRACY

Although piracy is considered the ultimate in lawlessness, it had its own moral code. At the outset of every voyage the pirates would swear to obey ship's rules, and infringements were punishable by whipping or walking the plank. A man who 'shall smoak Tobacco in the Hold without a cap to his Pipe', for example, would 'receive Moses' Law (that is 40 Stripes lacking one) on the bare Back'. And 'meddling' with a woman 'without her Consent' was punishable by death.

Mansell Collection

CHARACTERS IN FOCUS

Stevenson created larger-than-life characters who have become etched on to the public's imagination as the archetypal anti-heroes of sea-faring adventure. Ben Gunn, hovering between sanity and madness, and Long John Silver, with his combination of ruthlessness and charm, are two such extraordinary creations. Long John Silver haunts Jim's dreams "in a thousand forms, and with a thousand diabolical expressions" – and continues to fascinate generations of readers.

WHO'S WHO

Jim Hawkins   Narrator and hero, young Jim leaves home for a fabulous adventure.

The Captain (Billy Bones)   First mate to Captain Flint, Billy Bones receives the map of the treasure from Flint's dying hands, and then guards it, unsuccessfully, with his life.

Squire Trelawney   "Confoundedly hot-headed and exclamatory", the squire is benign but dangerously foolish.

Dr Livesey   "The neat, bright doctor . . . with his bright . . . eyes and pleasant manners" epitomizes decency and good sense.

Long John Silver   The most intelligent and cunning of the buccaneers, who is beguiling but also an "abominable old rogue".

Captain Smollett   Captain of the *Hispaniola*, his shrewdness and sound judgement prove invaluable.

Ben Gunn   A member of Flint's original crew, who has been living as half-man, half-beast on the island.

Israel Hands   The coxswain, "a careful, wily, old, experienced seaman", whose philosophy of life is that he has "never seen good come o' goodness yet".

Blind Pew   A "dreadful looking figure", Pew delivers the "black spot" warning to Captain Bill.

Black Dog   A former shipmate of Captain Bill whose appearance at the Admiral Benbow turns the captain "old and sick".

Bridgeman Art Library

Doctor Livesey (above) is brave, clear-sighted and a man to depend on. He is a strict moralist and believes, as he says to Jim, "as you have brewed, so shall you drink". He is not without compassion, however, and tends the pirates' ailments with the same diligence as he does those of his own men.

Mary Evans Picture Library

Fine Art Photographic Library

The enthusiasms of Squire Trelawney (left) are scarcely less boyish than Jim's, and once in possession of the map he wants to set off instantly. "Tomorrow I start for Bristol. In three weeks time – three weeks! – two weeks – ten days – we'll have the best ship, sir, and the choicest crew in England." The squire is taken in by Long John Silver and fails to recognize the worth of Captain Smollett. He is exasperating but likeable, and ready to confess himself an ass when events prove the error of his ways.

Long John Silver (left), though committed to villainy, is "no common man", and has to be admired for his bravery, his cunning and his charm. Even the level-headed doctor is taken in by him. Jim at first finds him "one of the best of possible shipmates", but discovers later "his cruelty, duplicity and power".

Single-minded in his desire for the treasure, Silver knows how to be patient, how to wait for the right moment and how to manipulate both friends and enemies.

An ordinary boy, leading a "quiet country life", Jim (below) gets the opportunity to live out every boy's (or girl's) fantasy of adventure and derring-do. He can hardly contain his excitement at going "to sea in a schooner, with a piping boatswain, and pig-tailed singing seamen; to sea, bound for an unknown island, and to seek for buried treasures." The experience, however, is a sobering one and casts a shadow on his youthful enthusiasms – the toll on lives is high and the island, once so magical, seems "accursed", the stuff not of dreams but of nightmares.

Chris Collingwood

"Gentlemen of fortune usually trusts little among themselves, and right they are", *Silver tells his fellow pirates* (above). And Israel Hands, Tom Morgan, Dick Johnson and George Merry prove about as trustworthy as Silver himself.

The "man of the island", Ben Gunn (right) appears both man and beast to young Jim. After three years away from civilization, this ragged creature is barely coherent. He has paid dearly for his desire for gold, possibly with his sanity.

Chris Collingwood

BOYHOOD HEROES

Inspired by his father's bedside tales of 'ships, roadside inns' and 'robbers', Stevenson went on to write classic, timeless adventure stories for 'children' of all ages.

Despite his success and versatility as a writer, Stevenson continually belittled his own talents. In 1885 he told the critic William Archer, 'I began with a neat brisk little style . . . I have tried to expand my means, but still I can only utter a part of what I wish to say, and am bound to feel; and much of it will die unspoken.' Nine years later, a few weeks before his death, he became depressed about the quality of his unfinished story *St Ives,* complaining to his friend Sidney Colvin that 'my skill deserts me, such as it is, or was . . . I cannot take myself seriously, as an artist the limitations are so obvious.' His 'very little dose of inspiration' and 'pretty little trick of style' had, he said, been 'improved by the most heroic industry'.

A DOGGED PROFESSIONAL

It is certainly true that, though frequently sick, Stevenson laboured at writing with the doggedness of a total professional, publishing 20 books in the last 16 years of his life. Novels, short stories, travel pieces, essays and poems flowed from his pen. In the vain hope of making a lot of money quickly, he collaborated in playwriting with his friend W. E. Henley. Later, mainly to help his stepson Lloyd Osbourne, the two worked together on the farcical story *The Wrong Box* and two 'South Sea Yarns', *The Wrecker* and *The Ebb-Tide.*

He wrote against the odds of sheer discomfort as well as illness. When crossing the Atlantic as a humble 'intermediate class' passenger, he finished a short story and made notes for *The Amateur Emigrant* as the ink bottle slid alarmingly from one side of his desk to the other. Stevenson told his stepson, 'What genius I had was for hard work.'

Nor did the creative act always come easily, as his own words reveal: 'But O, it has been such a grind! I break down at every paragraph . . . and lie here and sweat, till I can get one sentence wrung out after another'. At some point in the composition of every novel, he found himself unable to go on, and had to turn to some other project for a few weeks or months. As far as *The Master of Ballantrae* was concerned, this proved unfortunate, since Stevenson had sold the early chapters to *Scribner's Magazine* for serialization, and the need to finish the book plagued him all the way from Saranac to Honolulu. Though he did leave it aside for a time, his sense of being under pressure probably accounts for the falling off that most critics discern in the later part of the book. Because of his habit of laying projects aside, two of his novels, *St Ives* and *Weir of Hermiston*, were unfinished at his death.

By contrast, Stevenson often began a book with an extraordinary, inspirational flourish, as was the case with his first novel, *Treasure Island.* Stevenson enjoyed experimenting with Lloyd's paints, and 'On one of these occasions I made the map of an island; it was elaborately and (I thought) beautifully coloured: the shape of it took my fancy beyond expression; it contained harbours that pleased me like sonnets;

. . . as I pored over my map of Treasure Island, the future characters of the book began to appear there visibly among imaginary woods; and their brown faces and bright weapons peeped out upon me from unexpected quarters, as they passed to and fro, fighting, and hunting treasure. The next thing I knew I had some paper before me and was writing out a list of chapters. How often have I done so and the thing gone no farther! But there seemed elements of success about this enterprise.'

Indeed there were: Stevenson wrote 15 chapters in 15 days before he 'ignominiously lost hold'. Then, after a gap of a few weeks, he finished the book in a fortnight, during which the writing 'flowed from me like small talk' – which was just as well, since the story was being serialized in the magazine *Young Folks.*

Library of Congress, Washington

British Museum

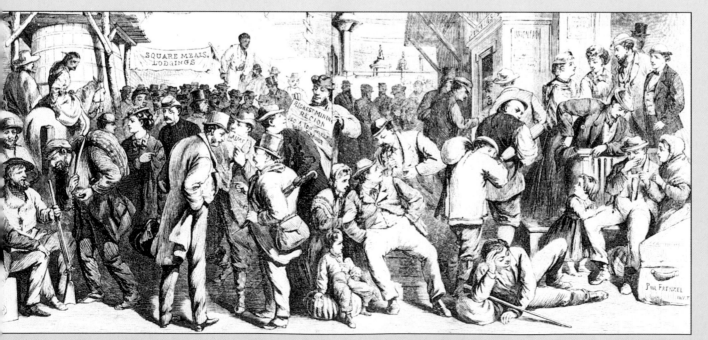

SQUARE MEALS, LODGINGS

Life into fiction
Stevenson used his exploits as material for his writing. The Silverado Squatters *(above) was based on his and Fanny's experiences of living in a silver miner's abandoned cottage. The Amateur Emigrant was an account of Stevenson's travels in crossing the Atlantic, then the United States (left) by train, in his pursuit of Fanny.*

Memories of Scotland

Like much of his best writing, The Master of Ballantrae *was 'conceived in Highland rain, in the blend of the smell of heather and bog plants'.*

The origin of *The Strange Case of Dr Jekyll and Mr Hyde* was even more remarkable. During the winter of 1884–5 Stevenson had a nightmare from which he was woken, screaming, by his wife Fanny. The following morning he began writing in bed, hardly stopping for three days. Then Stevenson read the completed 40,000-word tale to his family, as he did with all his works. Fanny's carping response – that the story should not be a mere thriller, but rather an allegory with a wider bearing on human existence – threw Stevenson into a rage. But when he had calmed down, he announced that she was right and flung the manuscript in the fire. Then he rewrote it in three days' furious work.

The Times praised Stevenson's 'very original genius' and called *Dr Jekyll and Mr Hyde* 'a finished study in the art of fantastic literature'. More importantly, it was a runaway success in both Britain and the United States.

Kidnapped started off more mundanely, with Stevenson researching 18th-century Scottish trials and finding much of his material in them. In fact 'I began it partly as a lark, partly as a pot-boiler; and suddenly it moved,

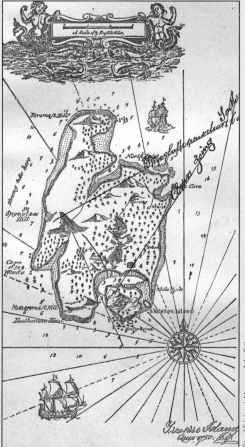

The birth of a masterpiece

Treasure Island *was inspired by a map that Stevenson drew to amuse his stepson Lloyd (below) as a boy. 'As I pored over my map . . . the future characters of the book began to appear there visibly among imaginary woods.' Such a map was to embellish the finished book (left).*

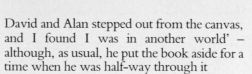

City of Edinburgh Museums & Art Galleries

'The story unfolds'

Stevenson dictated Weir of Hermiston *to his stepdaughter Belle (right), 'as clearly and steadily as though he were reading from some unseen book'. Like* The Master of Ballantrae *(above), it was set in Scotland – his final thoughts, though not his final home, being there.*

J. M. Barrie

Like Stevenson, J. M. Barrie (right) created child-heroes with whom he identified. Peter Pan was one such, shown above fighting the villainous Captain Hook. The two Scotsmen corresponded across the oceans, appraising each other's work.

Mary Evans Picture Library

David and Alan stepped out from the canvas, and I found I was in another world' – although, as usual, he put the book aside for a time when he was half-way through it

Kidnapped consolidated Stevenson's reputation as primarily a writer of historical romances, a wonderful storyteller, and an author of boys' books. All of this was true but, in addition, his insight into human life and character was complex and subtle.

Though an apparently straightforward escapist tale, *Treasure Island* contains at least one problematic character in Long John Silver. Generations of readers have responded to the lure of this murderous one-legged villain, who is at once devious, dangerous and undeniably charming. And *Dr Jekyll and Mr Hyde,* seemingly a plain allegory of good and evil, is in reality susceptible of many interpretations, including the message that repression of certain impulses may actually increase their potential strength.

In the Scottish novels, *Kidnapped* and *The Master of Ballantrae,* history represents the only certain force, and it becomes increasingly difficult for the reader to distinguish right from wrong, or the good man from the bad. Stevenson is the creator of adventure stories in which there are neither simple heroes nor easy choices, and this makes him a writer of a surprisingly modern kind.

Stevenson's writing was still developing when he died at 44. He was less than half-way through *Weir of Hermiston,* dictating it to his stepdaughter Belle Strong in order to avoid the writer's cramp from which he had suffered for years. 'Belle, I see it all so clearly!' he told her. 'The story unfolds itself before me to the least detail – there is nothing left in doubt. I never felt so before in anything I ever wrote. It will be my best work; I feel myself so sure of every word!' But the lovers' quarrel between Archie and Christina, dictated on the day of his death, was to be Stevenson's last contribution to literature.

Despite ill health, Robert Louis Stevenson worked prodigiously hard, and produced over 20 books. *Travels with a Donkey in the Cévennes* (1879) is an early example of the non-fictional travel narratives he published throughout his life. He also wrote essays, short stories and poems such as those in the enchanting *A Child's Garden of Verses* (1885). *Treasure Island* (1883) won him instant acclaim as a novelist. But the intriguing moral complexity of Stevenson's vision became apparent only on the publication of *The Strange Case of Dr Jekyll and Mr Hyde* (1886). *Kidnapped* (1886), a brilliant story of pursuit set against Scotland's turbulent history, was followed by the darker-toned *The Master of Ballantrae* (1889). This marked a step forward for the author, in his creation of character – the tension arises as much from the conflict between and within the characters as from the adventures that befall them. During his years on Samoa, Stevenson created fine South Seas tales, but his native land was never far from his thoughts. *Weir of Hermiston* (1896), a novel of 18th-century Scotland that is widely regarded as his masterpiece, lay unfinished at the time of his death.

KIDNAPPED
◆ 1886 ◆

A storm at sea (right) is one of the many exciting episodes in *Kidnapped*, perhaps the finest pursuit story ever written. It is said to be the 'Memoirs of the Adventures of David Balfour in the year 1751' – that is, soon after the Jacobite rebellion of 1745 had ended in disaster for the Highland clans that supported Bonnie Prince Charlie. The narrator is a Lowlander, 16-year-old David Balfour, who leaves home after his father's death, intending to claim his inheritance. His miserly and villainous Uncle Ebenezer reluctantly admits David to his queer, decaying home, the House of Shaws, and then tries to murder the boy in order to be the sole beneficiary of the Balfour Estate.

When the attempt fails, he arranges for David to be abducted and taken on to a ship, the *Covenant*, which is bound for the Carolinas in America. During the voyage, a fugitive Highland Jacobite, Alan Breck, is picked up from a sinking boat. The captain intends to kill Alan for the gold in his belt, but David warns him and helps him to fight off the crew. When the *Covenant* is wrecked off the coast of Mull, an island in the Inner Hebrides, David and Alan make a dangerous journey across Scotland, through territory still swarming with King George's redcoats.

Their troubles are increased when they witness the murder (a real historical event) of Colin Campbell, a factor (land-agent) to the king, and they are suspected of the crime. Despite their utterly dissimilar characters – David is a prim Lowlander, Alan a boastful, reckless Highlander – the two become close friends and help each other to survive and achieve their objectives.

Although highly popular, *Kidnapped* has never enjoyed quite the same renown as *Treasure Island*. It is, however, equal in narrative skill to the earlier novel, and adds an extra dimension in its evocation of the landscape and conflict-ridden history of Scotland.

In 1893 Stevenson published a sequel, *Catriona*, continuing the adventures of David Balfour. At great personal risk, David sets about absolving James Stewart of the Glens of Colin Campbell's murder. And he falls in love with Catriona Drummond, the daughter of a renegade. Alan Breck once again appears in the story – and makes a dramatic escape.

WEIR OF HERMISTON
◆ 1896 ◆

The dignity of the law (right) features strongly in Stevenson's last (unfinished) novel, of which he had completed nine chapters at the time of his death in 1894. In it he displays an astonishing new power and maturity – so much so that *Weir of Hermiston* has acquired a wide readership in spite of its fragmentary state. The central theme is the love-hate relationship between father and son. Adam Weir is a 'hanging judge', deeply learned in the law but brutal in speech and in meting out punishment to malefactors. Adam's earnest, sensitive son, Archie, challenges his father's views and is banished to the family estates at Hermiston. Here he falls in love with Christina Elliot, the housekeeper's neice, a proud girl who is alienated by Archie's prim insistence that they should stop meeting secretly for fear of scandal. When he had reached this point in the story, Stevenson died. He intended that Christina should be seduced by Frank Innes, one of Archie's college friends. Archie was to kill Innes in a fit of jealousy, and be tried by his own father, who has no alternative but to sentence him to death. It is likely, though not certain, that Stevenson would had allowed Archie to escape the gallows and make a new life in America with Christina, while Adam Weir dies of shock after the trauma of his son's trial. Both Christina and the other main female character in the book, her aunt Kirstie, are well-rounded and believable characters; this was the first time Stevenson had created such memorable women – a sign of his new maturity as a writer.

Raeburn: Portrait of Adam Rolland of Gask. (Detail). Bridgeman Art Library

TRAVELS WITH A DONKEY IN THE CÉVENNES
◆ 1879 ◆

Various incidents from this charming travel book (left) are compressed into one image in this engraving by Walter Crane, one of the most illustrious book illustrators of the 19th century. The heroine of the book is 'patient, elegant in form, the colour of an ideal mouse, and inimitably small'. She is Modestine, a donkey whom Stevenson purchases in the town of Le Monastier before setting out on a ten-day walk through the Cévennes, a remote highland region in southern France, the highest parts of which rise to well over 5000 feet.

Laden with the writer's awkward pack, the poor beast staggers slowly onwards, apparently on the point of collapse – until a peasant shows Stevenson how to wield a switch, whereupon Modestine's feminine frailty is revealed as a complete sham, and she forges ahead at a steady trot. Man and beast make their way through barren uplands to the Trappist monastery of Our Lady of the Snows, where they are hospitably received by the monks, although two boarders make strenuous attempts to convert Stevenson to Catholicism. After a memorable night under the stars in a pine wood, the travellers go down into a very different kind of country – the country of the Camisards, fierce Protestant guerrillas of earlier times, who in the early 18th century had revolted against the French government, and whose exploits, Stevenson discovers, are still alive in people's memories.

Finally, after so many shared experiences, Stevenson parts sorrowfully with Modestine and, as the stagecoach carries him away, 'I did not hesitate to yield to my emotion.' The journey had been undertaken to assuage his grief at being separated from his beloved Fanny, who was later to become his wife: 'I am damnably in love', he wrote at the time, and without Fanny it was 'damned hard work to keep up a good countenance'. This was the first time Stevenson had travelled without a human companion, but he met many people along the way and his sharply-drawn profiles of these characters, including inn-keepers and fellow travellers, form part of the book's appeal. *Travels with a Donkey* also contains some of the Stevenson's most beautiful poetic descriptions of Nature.

Mary Evans Picture Library

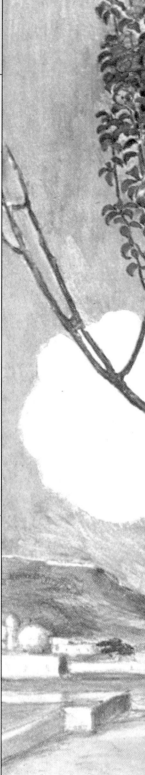

THE STRANGE CASE OF DR JEKYLL AND MR HYDE
✦ 1886 ✦

The interconnection of good and evil (below) is the central theme of this famous book. The friends of Henry Jekyll, a respected middle-aged doctor, are mystified by his intimate relationship with Edward Hyde, a man from whom most people instinctively shrink. But Jekyll insists that Hyde has been his benefactor, and even makes a will leaving all his possessions to this repellently 'pale and dwarfish' friend. The reason become clear only after some years, when Hyde commits a brutal murder. Subsequent events bring to light 'Henry Jekyll's Full Statement of the Case', a confession in which he admits to having experimented with drugs in order to separate the good and evil sides of his personality. His success has meant that, when he wishes, he can transform himself into Hyde, who 'alone in the ranks of mankind, was pure evil'. But Hyde has become so powerful that he can be kept at bay only by increasingly frequent doses of the drug. Feeling that he might be taken over completely, Jekyll has made a will in Hyde's favour. But with Hyde a hunted man and supplies of the drug running out, there is only one way in which the desperate doctor can terminate the career of his evil other self . . . Combining the qualities of a thrilling scientific fantasy and a powerful moral fable, *Dr Jekyll and Mr Hyde* is one of the most famous of all novels and has enjoyed enormous success and popularity. It sold 40,000 copies in the first six months, Queen Victoria being among the readers whose imagination it caught. It was taken as the theme for sermons and articles in religious newspapers, and it has found an increasingly wide audience as the subject of numerous stage and film versions. The basic idea of the macabre transformation came to Stevenson in a nightmare during which he screamed so loudly that his wife had to wake him. The finished book, however, was the second version Stevenson wrote, since the first made too little capital out of the storyline's philosophical and allegorical potential.

Arnold Böcklin: Self-Portrait with Death Playing the Fiddle. (Detail). Nationalgalerie, Staatliche Museen Preussischer Kulturbesitz

A CHILD'S GARDEN OF VERSES
✦ 1885 ✦

Idyllic childhood images (above) fill this delightful collection of light verse. The poems were mainly written at Nice and Hyères, where Stevenson was often too ill for the extended effort needed to write fiction. *A Child's Garden* evokes the timeless world of childhood, but it is also profoundly autobiographical. It is dedicated to Stevenson's nurse, Alison Cunningham, 'from her boy', and includes poignant memories of 'picture story-books', 'When I was sick and lay a-bed'. Stevenson conjures up images of himself as a little boy who fancied he could climb a tree and look out on to foreign lands, and – prophetically – imagines himself travelling to places 'Where below another sky/Parrot islands anchored lie'. The autobiographical element makes the collection quite different from most anthologies for children.

Edinburgh Life

Cold and austere, colourful and squalid, Edinburgh both repelled and attracted Stevenson. Its climate drove him in search of balmy sunshine, but time and distance only heightened its fascination.

Stevenson spent much of his life travelling for the sake of his health, but the place that most vividly affected his imagination was his native city of Edinburgh. In 1882 he wrote to his friend Charles Baxter from the South of France, recalling their youthful escapades: 'O for ten Edinburgh minutes, sixpence between us and the ever glorious Lothian Road, or dear mysterious Leith Walk.' And even when he was half the globe away in the South Seas he wrote nostalgically of what he called the 'precipitous city'.

Wandering around Edinburgh's steep banks and handsome stone-faced streets today it requires only a small effort of the imagination to be carried back to 1850, the year of Stevenson's birth. In spite of slum clearance and rebuilding, Edinburgh has probably changed less in essentials during the past two centuries than any other capital city in Europe. It is a small place compared with most of the others and (not being a seat of government) more remote from political affairs.

A SPLENDID ERA

Even in the mid-19th century, Edinburgh was a city living on its memory – the memory of the resplendent age in the late 18th century when it had earned the name 'the Athens of the North'. This description referred not only to the Grecian purity of the architecture of the Georgian New Town, but also to the cultural and intellectual flowering that took place at this time. It was the city's heyday in art and literature, when it boasted painters like Allan Ramsay and Sir Henry Raeburn, and

A bustling city
(below and left) The Old Town of Edinburgh was crowded and busy in Stevenson's day, the streets animated by colourful characters. Below left is a square in front of the ancient church of St Giles, but much more typical of this picturesequely squalid area is the tenement scene inset, with washing fluttering from the windows in the manner described by Stevenson in his Edinburgh, Picturesque Notes, *a lively account of the city published in 1878.*

Doyle. The Winning Shot. City of Edinburgh Museums & Art Galleries

Mary Evans Picture Library

heroes of the Enlightenment such as the philosopher David Hume and the political economist Adam Smith. It was also a time when the English gentry sent their sons to Edinburgh's renowned university.

These things represented only one aspect of Edinburgh, however. As Stevenson wrote, 'Few places, if any, offer a more barbaric display of contrasts to the eye.' He was referring to the remarkable diversity of natural and architectural features that Edinburgh presents within a small compass, from the rugged splendour of the castle on its rock – 'one of the most satisfactory crags in nature' – to the towering tenements, like 'smokey beehives ten stories high', and from the picturesque but squalid Old Town to the New Town's 'open squares and gardens of the wealthy'.

Edinburgh's pleasures
Although Edinburgh was noted for its bad weather and had a reputation for smoky gloom (below), it was a convivial place. Curling, a winter sport associated chiefly with Scotland, drew all classes of society to the ice of Duddingston Loch (above left), and the Advocates' Library (above) was one of several splendid reading rooms that added to the city's attractions.

the wind whistles through the town as if it were an open window.'

The greyness seemed particularly appropriate on Sundays, for Edinburgh was as conservative and formal a city in its manners as in its architecture. In the New Town, where Stevenson passed his boyhood, the older professions, represented by genteel families from the Church, the Law and the armed services, preserved the old Scottish Sabbath. On this day a harsh discipline kept respectable folk indoors, quiet and immobile behind thick curtains, while church bells moaned their ancient dissonances across empty, windswept streets.

The new rich had left the New Town for the Victorian villas, which in Stevenson's time were stretching in suburbs towards the eastern coast, for although the

WINTRY GLOOM

Over the Old Town in Stevenson's day hung the drifting cloud of smoke that gave the city the name of 'Auld Reekie'. Grime attached itself to the stone and added its patina to the blend of innumerable greys for which Edinburgh is famous – grey rock merging in winter with grey watery sky. It can create a lovely sight, but the young, delicate Stevenson shivered in what he called 'one of the vilest climates under the heaven':

'To none but those who have themselves suffered the thing in the body, can the gloom and depression of our Edinburgh winters be brought home. For some constitutions there is something almost physically disgusting in the bleak ugliness of easterly weather; the wind wearies, the sickly sky depresses them . . . The days are so short that a man does much of his business, and certainly all his pleasure, by the haggard glare of gas lamps. The roads are as heavy as a fallow. People go by, so drenched and draggle-tailed that I have often wondered how they found the heart to undress. And meantime

Mary Evans Picture Library

Walter Geikie: A Hallow Fair Scene. City of Edinburgh Musuems & Art Galleries

James Hare. City of Edinburgh Museums & Art Galleries

Edinburgh fairs

(above and right) Edinburgh is famous for its grey-stoned architectural dignity, but in Stevenson's time a vivid note of colour was supplied by the various fairs that went on in its streets and nearby. Above is a delightful collection of quirky characters at a fair on the outskirts of the city, and on the right is an amazingly energetic scene at the Horse Fair in the Grassmarket, with the Castle in the background.

centre of Edinburgh changed little, there was great expansion in the outlying areas. During the 19th century the population of the city grew from under 100,000 to about 400,000. Essentially that was a native growth, for Edinburgh has never enjoyed the sudden bursts of prosperity that have brought strangers swarming in, nor the sudden economic setbacks that drive people out of a city.

Subject neither to bouts of emigration nor immigration, Edinburgh had, as it has still today, the most indigenous population of any major city in United Kingdom – hence, perhaps, the domesticity of the place, and the tolerant mix of social classes. On the ice of Duddingston Loch it was an everyday event to find minister and judge, poacher and farmhand meeting together in easy familiarity to contest a curling match. By Stevenson's time the division between the classes was no doubt becoming sharper, though it would be rash to accept his verdict that 'social inequality is nowhere more ostentatious than at Edinburgh'.

Just as Georgian Edinburgh had reluctantly aban-

Calton Jail

(right) Edinburgh's most famous prison was the Tolbooth, nicknamed the Heart of Midlothian, but this is the more modern jail at the bottom of Calton Hill. Stevenson was familiar with prison interiors, as he visited his low-life friends when they were in jail.

doned the sedan chair for the coach, so Victorian Edinburgh replaced the coach by the horse tram (which first appeared in 1871), but fundamental change was less drastic than elsewhere. Edinburgh escaped the worst consequences of the Industrial Revolution, for its industries were mainly light and clean, its economic importance depending more on its role as the centre of Scottish banking and insurance.

SQUALOR AND VICE

Being free of the 'mass employment' of northern English towns, Edinburgh was also unvisited by 'mass unemployment'. The gulf between master and man, capital and labour, was also less evident than it was in Bolton or Bradford. But the gap between rich and poor widened and became more noticeable. The old convivial life of the tavern, which in an earlier age had been as much a part of Edinburgh as its law courts, churches and assembly rooms, and which had brought together people of all ranks and incomes in a genuinely democratic friendship, was by 1850 a fading institution, conquered by prosperity and Victorian notions of refinement and 'respectability'. The public house was driven morally and socially underground and drinking itself, even the drinking of whisky, was, if not obliterated,

transformed into a domestic weakness or a private vice.

In the Old Town of Edinburgh there was squalor as well as vice. The St Giles quarter, washed with rain the year through and bearing a grim and sooty aspect, was a broken-down district of dank arches and dark stairs. Here whole families of the new urban poor huddled in airless one-roomed hovels, washing fluttering from every window. Stevenson wrote of 'an air of sluttishness and dirt' and of 'broken shutters, wry gables, old palsied houses on the brink of ruin, a crumbling human pigsty fit for pigs'. By the Heart of Midlothian (the nickname for Edinburgh's prison), under the ancient Market Cross, fishwives sold oysters and whelks from Newhaven and Musselburgh, and a stray caddie (or messenger) from a grander age might be seen touting for custom among the legal clerks. But drunkenness, thievery and prostitution were the most salient marks of the district, which was now almost entirely segregated from the society of the fashionable New Town.

Dr George Bell, writing in 1850 of his investigations into the health and living conditions of the city's poor, expressed his horror of the scenes he witnessed daily. 'From the toothless infant to the toothless old man, the population of the wynds [narrow alleys] drinks whisky. The drunken drama that is enacted on Satur-

Fleshmarket Close

(above) Vice was rife in the dingy, decaying streets of Edinburgh's Old Town, and prostitution was a fact of everyday life. In the aptly named Fleshmarket Close, several of the women who stand at doors or appear at windows are probably ladies of easy virtue.

A haunting city
Stevenson had many unpleasant things to say about Edinburgh, but deep in his heart he had an enduring love for the city. This view from the castle hill over the rooftops shows the rugged beauty that haunted his imagination.

day night and Sabbath morning beggars description.'

Overcrowding was at a shocking level and sanitation primitive. Dr H. D. Littlejohn, the city's first Medical Officer of Health, published a *Report on the Sanitary Conditions of the City of Edinburgh* (1865) in which he highlighted such appalling conditions, saying 'that with the possible exception of some districts of Liverpool, in no part of the world does there exist greater overcrowding of population'. Littlejohn's recommendations for improving public health included regular inspection of cow byres (there were still many of these in courts and closes in the city), the lifting of manure every week (instead of every fortnight), and compulsory introduction of toilets into the houses of the poor. During the 1860s sanitary conditions were considerably improved by the widespread installation of sewers in the city.

DELIGHTS OF THE FLESH

Away from the ugly, demeaning poverty of St Giles, members of Edinburgh's underworld spent their nights and early mornings among the new Victorian surburbs on the eastern slopes of the city. Indeed, the delights of the flesh gained added piquancy from being stolen at the very heart of the conservative, puritan capital of Scotland. It was those streets which Stevenson had in his mind's eye when he wrote the lines,

I love the night in the City,
The lighted streets and the swinging gait of harlots.

There he sat as a youth, open-eyed, in thieves' kitchens; there were the all-night underground or 'back-of-the-house' supper and drinking rooms; and there, too, the dance halls breathed an intemperate vitality all night long and were a living contradiction of the Glaswegian's taunt (mocking both the prudery and the Anglicized accent of well-to-do Edinburgh) that in the capital sex was what coal was delivered in.

In haunting these disreputable places as a young man, Stevenson was rebelling against the strict values of his upbringing, and his experiences must have had a powerful effect on his imagination, acquainting him with a rich variety of low-life characters. He always carried a note-book with him to record his impressions, and no doubt the low places haunted by Mr Hyde and the coarse-grained villains in *Treasure Island* were at least partly inspired by the sights and sounds of Stevenson's inquisitive youth.

His attitudes towards his native city were summed up in his book *Edinburgh, Picturesque Notes,* published in 1878. Much of what he said was far from complimentary, and he offended some citizens by his remarks about their materialism and ultra-respectability (he noted that the offence was balanced by giving 'a proportionable pleasure to our rivals of Glasgow'). Yet however much he complained about the city of his birth, his most abiding response to it was one of love:

'The weather is raw and boisterous in winter, shifty and ungenial in summer, and downright meteorological purgatory in the spring. The delicate die early, and I, as a survivor, among bleak winds and plumping rain, have been sometimes tempted to envy them their fate. For all who love shelter and the blessings of the sun, who hate dark weather and perpetual tilting against squalls, there could scarcely be found a more unhomely and harassing place of residence. . . They lean over the great bridge which joins the New Town with the Old – and watch the trains smoking out from under them and vanishing into the tunnel on a voyage to brighter skies. Happy the passengers who shake off the dust of Edinburgh, and have heard for the last time the cry of the east wind among her chimney-tops! And yet the place establishes an interest in people's hearts; go where they will, they find no city of the same distinction; go where they will, they take a pride in their old home.'

RUDYARD KIPLING

◆1865-1936◆

Rudyard Kipling has always been a controversial figure. He
was dubbed by Henry James 'the most complete man of genius
I have ever known', and dismissed by George Orwell as 'a
jingo-imperialist . . . morally insensitive and aesthetically
disgusting'. Yet he has never ceased to delight a vast readership
with his brilliant verse and prose, and his stories for children are
some of the finest ever written. Kipling's acknowledged
masterpiece is an unforgettable portrait of India – *Kim*.

FOR LOVE OF EMPIRE

Born in India at the height of the British Empire, Kipling championed the virtues of loyalty to Queen and Country to become one of the most eminent Englishmen of his time.

Kipling has become in the British consciousness virtually a personification of the country's former Empire. He supported and celebrated the Empire with lifelong zeal. But there is much more to Kipling than his imperialism – his love for children and admiration for the 'common man' inspired some of the best-loved stories and verses of all time.

Joseph Rudyard Kipling was born in Bombay on 30 December 1865. His unusual name derived from Lake Rudyard (now Rudyard Reservoir) in Staffordshire, where his parents, John Lockwood Kipling and Alice Macdonald, met on a picnic. In 1865, three months after their marriage, they sailed to India, where John had been appointed Professor of Architectural Sculpture at the newly founded Bombay School of Art.

Although they were not wealthy, the Kiplings had a much better lifestyle than they would have enjoyed in England, with the young Rudyard (or Ruddy as he was sometimes known) being pampered by the household servants. But when he was nearly six Rudyard was abruptly removed from this privileged, exotic world and sent to live with strangers in bleak, blustery Southsea, thousands of miles away on the Hampshire coast.

British settlers in India believed that the British way of life was the best, and that children had to be immersed in the culture of their home country and safeguarded from the numerous fatal diseases in India. Children were customarily sent home to live with relations or, failing that, with families who undertook to foster them, for a fee.

CRUEL DESOLATION

Since Rudyard was apparently too difficult for his relations to handle, Alice opted for the Southsea home, which she found in an advertisement. Without explaining what was happening to Rudyard or his younger sister Trix, she took them back to England in 1871. They stayed at Lorne Lodge with 'Uncle Harry' and 'Aunty Rosa' (Captain and Mrs Holloway) for the next six years, estranged from their parents, who could not afford the time and the cost of the journey.

Life was tolerable to begin with, largely because Captain Holloway liked Rudyard and kept a check on his wife's harsh temperament, but when he

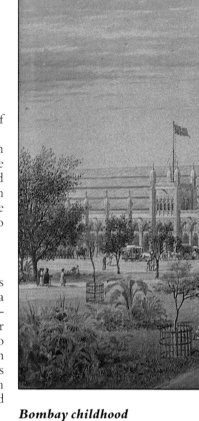

Bombay childhood
(above) Born into the relative luxury of an English family abroad, Kipling spent the first six years of his life among the exotic wonders of Bombay.

Loving parents
Rudyard's father, shown far left in a book-label of his own design, taught at the Bombay School of Art. His talent was put to use in collaboration with his son, for he illustrated Kim *and other works with his low-relief sculptures. Alice, Rudyard's mother, was tender and affectionate, and was also noted for her witty tongue. Kipling loved both parents, and after his father's death he referred to him as 'a great man'.*

EX LIBRIS

FUMUS GLORIA MUNDI

JOHN LOCKWOOD KIPLING

Weidenfeld Archive

Weidenfeld Archive

died everything changed. Lorne Lodge became Kipling's 'House of Desolation'.

Unlike his sister, Rudyard could do nothing right, and was constantly being punished and locked in his room. There was even a ban on reading, his greatest passion, resulting in furtive sessions in poor light nearly ruining his already weak eyesight. The worst indignity was being sent to school with the placard 'Liar' stitched to his coat. In six years he was reduced from a healthy, robust little boy to a state of constant insecurity. When his mother returned in 1877 to collect him, and bent down for a kiss, his lightning response was to duck as if about to be hit.

DISAPPOINTED SCHOLAR

Years later Kipling recounted the horrors of this period in *The Light That Failed*, *Baa, Baa, Black Sheep* and his autobiography, *Something of Myself*, though it is hard to discover how much he exaggerated. It is quite possible, however, that the Southsea experience gave him his near mystical love for children, prompting his delight at reading his own stories to them.

Kipling's education continued with a four-year spell at a Devon college, Westward Ho!, which was primarily geared to sending its students into the army. It introduced Kipling to the world of action, which later became a vital ingredient of his literary works, and allowed him to develop a taste for literature. But Rudyard did not stay on for a full upper-class 'English education'. This left him

House of Desolation
Lorne Lodge, Southsea (below), his foster home in England, drove young Rudyard (right) to despair.

Key Dates

1865 born in Bombay

1871 taken to England to 'adoptive' family

1882 returns to India as a journalist

1889 returns to England

1892 marries Caroline Balestier

1892-96 in America

1896-1902 lives on S.E. coast of England

1899 death of daughter, Josephine

1900 first visit to South Africa

1901 *Kim* published

1907 awarded the Nobel Prize

1915-1918 visits naval and army bases

1915 death of son in World War I

1917 invited to work with War Graves Commission

1936 dies in London

EDWARD BURNE-JONES

Apart from his father, Kipling had two uncles who were also artists – Sir Edward Burne-Jones and Sir Edward Poynter. Both were highly distinguished in their time and Burne-Jones remains one of the most celebrated of Victorian painters. He was particularly close to his nephew as a youth, when Kipling was lonely as a 'hermit crab'.

Pre-Raphaelite master
Burne-Jones specialized in dreamy evocations of a romantic medieval world – inhabited by beautiful maidens.

Sir Edward Burne-Jones The Mirror of Venus Gulbenkian Foundation, Lisbon/Bridgeman Art Library

with a chip on his shoulder, and he said of his cousin (the future Prime Minister, Stanley Baldwin), 'I'd give anything to be in the Sixth [final year] at Harrow as he is, with a university education to follow'. Instead, his father had got Rudyard a job on an English newspaper in India.

Kipling was 16 when he returned to India in 1882. He worked extremely hard at his job, 'never less than 10 hours, and seldom more than 15'. Eventually he wrote weekly articles, most of which were reprinted in his first prose book, *Plain Tales from the Hills* (1888). Around this time Kipling gained his first experience of what it was like to be politically controversial. On entering his club in Lahore (now in Pakistan) the members booed him, though not for anything he had written. In their eyes he was the paper's representative, whose liberal views were not welcome.

TRAVELS IN THE ORIENT

All the while Kipling was rapidly becoming an important literary figure in India, and at the age of 24 he decided it was time to leave his Indian outpost and take on literary London. Save for one visit, this was the last time he saw India, but his time there permanently affected his outlook and his writings. It gave him a landscape and cast of characters for some of his finest works, and the view which became the cornerstone of his political philosophy – that the only force keeping back anarchy was the Empire.

On 9 March 1889 Kipling started a long voyage home, beginning with a three-months' trip to San

'Joyous home-coming'
In 1882, not yet 17, Kipling returned to India, this time to Lahore (right), to parents he had barely seen for 11 years: 'the mother proved more delightful than all my imaginings or memories. My father was not only a mine of knowledge and help, but a humorous, tolerant and expert fellow craftsman.' In his new post of journalist, Kipling had a servant, horse, cart and groom. Three times a week, the English of Lahore gathered to play tennis, dance and socialize. Nevertheless, Kipling worked 10 to 15 hours a day, six days a week, he and his boss producing by themselves the only daily paper in the Punjab.

Francisco via Burma, Malaya, Hong Kong and Japan. The trip gave him a love of cruises, which later became a near-annual palliative against anxiety and ill health. It also sharpened his world view. Not only were the Indians the white man's cultural poor relations, so too were the Chinese, though he treated them more severely, revealing the most unpalatable side of his imperialism. In *From Sea to Sea* (1899), a collection of Kipling's travel letters, he wrote: 'It is justifiable to kill him [the Chinaman]. It would be quite right to wipe the city of Canton off the face of the earth.'

GUNBOAT DIPLOMACY

Kipling's harsh opinions on other countries extended to the United States, and when he sailed into San Francisco he made the infamous remark that there was no need to worry because a couple of British gunboats could easily take the place! His views on the United States soon became ambivalent, however. While he despaired of the inhabitants' clothes, lack of manners, lawlessness, boasting and tendency to spit, he also relished the climate, the free and confident women, and the spectacular scenery.

When Kipling reached England in October 1889 he found his reputation had preceded him. Now he sent it soaring. He wrote consistently well, producing *Barrack-Room Ballads* (offending and delighting many with his ripe vernacular) and some

T. Longcroft Palace at Lahore Victoria & Albert Museum/Bridgeman Art Library

excellent short stories, winning many good reviews, with one in *The Times* crowning him 'the discoverer of India'. His private life was also flourishing: he had recently fallen in love with Caroline 'Carrie' Balestier, his agent's sister.

However, events quickly turned against him. His novel *The Light that Failed* (1890) was a flop, and this, combined with overwork and bad health from various Indian fevers, produced such anxiety

Newlyweds' home
After Kipling married Caroline Balestier (right), they set off round the world, ending in Vermont, New England, Carrie's home, where they built a house called Naulakha (above).

Bikanir House
The Kiplings' white bungalow in Lahore was set in its own compound empty of bushes. The family hoped thus to deter insects, which they believed spread disease. Because of this wasteland, neighbours nicknamed the house 'Bikanir', after the Indian desert.

that he fled the country after just two years. He made for Australia and the Far East but soon after his departure heard that his agent had died. Kipling dashed back to be with Carrie, arriving on 10 January 1892. They were married eight days later.

The Kiplings took a round-the-world honeymoon, stopping off in Vermont in the north eastern United States to visit Carrie's parents. Kipling was so excited by the surrounding countryside and its inhabitants that they stayed for four years. They bought some land next to Carrie's family's home, built a house and had a child, Josephine.

FAMILY CONFLICTS

Before they reached the United States, however, they had visited Japan, where Kipling lost his money in a banking collapse, prompting Carrie to take charge of their finances and household management. Kipling benefited from this arrangement in many ways, since it left him free in Vermont to write some of his finest works, including *The Jungle Books*. Yet with Carrie now permanently in charge of their affairs he felt reduced to 'no more than a cork on the water', his life circumscribed by her organization. But if there was a potential for conflict, it never arose; that was saved for the Kiplings' relationship with Carrie's sharp-tongued, penniless, drunken brother Beatty.

Relationships between the two households disintegrated from 1894, culminating in Beatty's threat to kill Kipling. Kipling and Carrie called in the local sheriff, taking Beatty to court. However, according to Carrie, it was Kipling who was left 'a total wreck'. The press had a field day at the great English author's expense and, though a verdict was held over to the next session, the Kiplings had had enough and returned to England.

From 1896 to 1902 they lived briefly in Torquay, then at Rottingdean, a quaint coastal village near Brighton. Kipling was as productive as ever, writing the *Just So* stories and shrewd political items about the threat from Germany and the likelihood of European war. But his life was soon shattered by a more private tragedy.

COLD DEATH

In the winter of 1898-99, the Kiplings went on an American trip to visit Carrie's parents. Despite warnings that the weather was too severe for the children (they now had two girls and a boy) they proceeded with their plan. Sadly the warnings came true. Once in the United States, Kipling went down with severe pneumonia in both lungs, the children with fever. The writer's near-fatal condition became daily front-page news, with reporters besieging his rooms. He even got a 'Get Well' message from the Kaiser.

Kipling eventually recovered, but Josephine did not. Carrie had to keep the news of her death from him until days after the burial, when he was strong enough to take it. Kipling never returned to the United States, and never recovered from this tragedy. Carrie's strength of character pulled him through the following months. *They*, published in 1904, is one of the few works, albeit indirectly, to

Bateman's, The National Trust

'. . . it's all our own!'
(above) The Jacobean mansion Bateman's, at Burwash in Sussex, was Kipling's home for the last 34 years of his life. Friends found it damp and depressing, but Kipling delighted in its stately grandeur and extensive grounds 'including a mill which was paying taxes in 1296!'

tackle the heart-rending subject of Josephine's death.

Kipling's time at Rottingdean coincided with the Boer War (1899-1902). Always excited by war, he travelled to South Africa to check the military hospitals and ensure the British troops were being properly cared for. Their condition was woeful. In addition to the fighting they had to contend with typhoid, dysentery and their bungling commanders. Kipling devoted himself to working with the wounded and writing letters home for the most severely disabled. He also produced a newspaper for the troops.

Back home in Rottingdean, he did everything he could to raise the villagers to his own pitch of excitement. He fired a cannon over the cliff's edge to welcome home three local soldiers, and later went through the streets loudly rattling tin cans to celebrate the Relief of Mafeking.

Max Beerbohm: Kipling & Britannia: Mrs Eva Reichmann/British Library

By jingo!
(left) Kipling's popular image is summed up in this cartoon. Champion of vernacular speech, jingoistic patriot, he became almost a caricature of Empire – an image that went against him when the tide of popular opinion later turned away from imperialism.

THE BESIEGED LAUREATE

Kipling was the self-appointed Laureate of the Empire. His friend Cecil Rhodes, the founder of Rhodesia, described him as having 'done more than any other since Disraeli to show the world that the British race is sound at core and that rust and dry rot are strangers to it'. His politics made him a controversial figure and literary critics were often unenthusiastic about his work. But the general reading public adored him. Consequently Kipling's home, all too accessible on the village green, came to be peered at and surrounded by the

Loved and lost
(left inset) Kipling's three children, from left to right, Elsie, John and Josephine, were a source of great, unqualified joy: he spoiled them shamelessly. After Josephine – 'the child that was all to him' – died, he wrote, 'People say that kind of wound heals. It doesn't'. Added to that wound was John's death in World War I, after which Kipling sank into a deep pessimism from which he never recovered.

ZAM-ZAMMAH

*K*im opens with the hero sitting on the barrel of this great bronze cannon outside the 'Wonder House' – Lahore Museum. Kipling knew the scene well, for his father was curator of the museum.

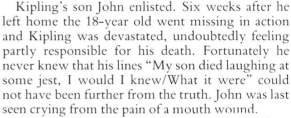

increasing numbers of curious south-coast tourists.

In 1902 the family moved to Bateman's, a Jacobean house at Burwash, a well-wooded part of the Sussex Weald. The last of his Eastern stories, including *Kim*, were completed at Rottingdean. After the move his fiction took on a wider dimension, partly inspired by the new landscape. In 1907 Kipling won the Nobel Prize for Literature.

Unhappy times were to follow. Many good friends died, Kipling's health began to suffer and, in 1914, as he had been fearing, Europe was plunged into the most horrific war in its history.

King and Trumpeter
By the 1920s, Kipling was a household name – a literary giant and a national figurehead. He is pictured left with King George V, visiting war graves in Belgium in 1922, in his capacity as advisor to the War Graves Commission. The two men became quite friendly, and when they died within a few days of each other – Kipling on his own 44th wedding anniversary – it was said the King had sent his Trumpeter ahead of him.

Kipling's son John enlisted. Six weeks after he left home the 18-year old went missing in action and Kipling was devastated, undoubtedly feeling partly responsible for his death. Fortunately he never knew that his lines "My son died laughing at some jest, I would I knew/What it were" could not have been further from the truth. John was last seen crying from the pain of a mouth wound.

Kipling's standing after the war was as high as ever. The Prime Minister offered him any honour he wanted, but Kipling was not interested in accepting titles. He turned down the Order of Merit three times and also the poet laureateship, but he was awarded (without his permission) a Companionship of Honour. He continued writing, but his works became increasingly sombre.

PAINFUL ILLNESSES

In his early fifties Kipling began to suffer terrible pains, which went undiagnosed for nearly 20 years, until he was found to have duodenal ulcers. He was well cared for by Carrie, but depressed at the extent to which she over-protected him, and by her parsimonious household management. At its most excessive this extended to switching off the electricity whenever they went away, distributing candles and matches to the unfortunate remaining servants. In 1930, Carrie also fell ill, crippled by rheumatism and attacked by diabetes.

The same year, the Kiplings took a much-needed holiday to Bermuda, and a trip to Egypt. Despite old age the author's mind still teemed with ideas. Also, his belief in the 'English Spirit' was as strong as ever, though he now felt increasingly out of place in a Britain where ideas of imperialism were being questioned. France became the country outside England on which he focused his hopes, and he often holidayed there.

In 1934 Kipling wrote his autobiography *Something of Myself*. Two years later, while setting out for a winter break in Cannes, he had a severe haemorrhage in London. He died four days later, on 18 January 1936. His ashes rest in Poets' Corner, Westminster Abbey.

KIM

A holy man from Tibet and a young Irish boy travel through India. One is searching for spiritual redemption, the other for adventure, which he finds in the 'Great Game' – espionage.

*K*im has been described as the best picture of India by an English author. It is an unforgettable, magical portrayal of the land and its people, as seen through the eyes of an old Tibetan lama and a young British boy who have been thrown into each other's path and who take to the road together. To Kim, this encounter with the colour and castes of India is all excitement. To the lama, it is all illusion. The novel is not only about the British in India: it is about different ways of seeing life.

GUIDE TO THE PLOT

Although the son of an Irish soldier, Kimball O'Hara, Kim lives like an Indian in Lahore (then India, now Pakistan) speaking "the vernacular by preference", and looking as "black as any native". Sitting "in defiance of municipal orders" on a

Kim O'Hara
(left) Squatting "knees to chin", and dressed like "a Hindu urchin in a dirty turban", Kim is scarcely recognizable as a white "sahib". But his destiny lies with the British.

cannon outside Lahore Museum, Kim catches sight of a man "nearly six feet high, dressed in fold upon fold of dingy stuff like horse-blanketing, and not one fold of it could Kim refer to any known trade or profession". This is Kim's first vision of the lama, the holy man from Tibet, and the man's strange appearance immediately appeals to Kim's incorrigible curiosity.

Following the lama into Lahore Museum, he discovers that the holy man is searching for the sacred River, which will "wash away all taint and speckle of sin" and free him from the Wheel of Life. Kim offers to become the lama's *chela* (disciple) and help him in his Search, for it is clear that the lama has very little idea how to take care of himself.

Kim is intrigued by the lama's eccentricity and obsession with finding the River, because Kim too has a destiny. Parchment, paper and birth certificate have been sewn into a leather amulet-case which Kim wears around his neck, and he has been told that "there will come for you a great Red Bull on a green field, and the Colonel riding on his tall horse . . ." Kim senses a possible kinship between the old man's search and his own.

Prior to setting out on their journey, Kim is entrusted with a message about a

white stallion's pedigree by the horse-trader, Mahbub Ali, who wishes him to deliver it to a British officer in Umballa. In doing so, Kim confirms his impression that the message has less to do with horses than with intelligence work, and it gives

Marianne North: The bazaar in Ajmer. Royal Botanic Gardens, Kew

The journey begins
Kim and the lama start their journey at Lahore's railway station. The lama is terrified of the "te-rains" – "the work of Devils!". He is the sage but Kim has the worldlier wisdom.

Reproduced by permission of Punch

Reproduced by permission of Punch

At the bazaar
Coming from an isolated monastery in Tibet, the lama is stunned by the bustling, crowded bazaars of Northern India (left). But not so Kim.

Begging for food
(right) As the lama's chela (disciple), Kim takes responsibility for begging for them both. In Tibet, holy men beg in silence, but as Kim remarks, in India, "Those who beg in silence starve in silence."

On the road
On the Grand Trunk Road (below) Kim and the lama first meet an old Kulu woman from the Himalayas in a "family bullock-cart, with broidered canopy of two domes, like a double-humped camel".

"The morning mist swept off in a whorl of silver, the parrots shot away to some distant river in shrieking green hosts: all the well-wheels within ear-shot went to work. India was awake, and Kim was in the middle of it . . ."

J. Griffiths: A Drink by the Way. Victoria & Albert Museum/Bridgeman Art Library

him his first glimpse of the British officer, Colonel Creighton, who is to play an important role in young Kim's life.

On the road with the lama, Kim sees two soldiers planting a flag and notices that the design is of a "great Red Bull on a background of Irish green" – actually the emblem of his father's regiment, the Mavericks. When he investigates further, he is apprehended by the two clergymen of the regiment, Mr Bennett and Father Victor. Kim is recognized as O'Hara's son, and he and the lama are temporarily separated when Kim is sent to St Xavier's school in Lucknow – "the very school and discipline he had spent two-thirds of his young life avoiding".

However, with the aid of Mahbub Ali, Kim is introduced to Colonel Creighton, of the British Secret Service, who has a network of spies reporting back on any subversive activity in outlying regions. While Kim's education continues, the Colonel often thinks of "the queer, silent, self possessed boy. His evasion of course, was the height of insolence, but it argued some resource and nerve."

On the advice of Mahbub Ali, the Colonel is already thinking of introducing

Kim to the "Great Game" – spying for the British. When Kim journeys to Simla, he will meet Lurgan Sahib, who will school him in the art of disguise and deception.

In the meantime, the lama has been helping to finance Kim's education and

On the road

Bateman's, The National Trust

"coming and going across India as softly as a bat". He and Kim are reunited and together they renew the search for the sacred River. Noticing the change in Kim and observing his proficiency at the Great Game, the lama comments that "thou

Escape from school
To escape in disguise from St Xavier's school, Kim persuades a local dancing girl to dye his skin and dress him as a low-caste Hindu. His skill in disguise proves useful later.

The Holy City
(right) The ancient city of Benares on the Ganges is one of the holiest places in India. Here the lama waits for Kim who "acquires wisdom" at St Xavier's.

hast acquired great wisdom. Beware that it do not give birth to pride."

With the help of the Bengali, Hurree Babu – and, inadvertently, the lama – Kim assists in the Great Game by foiling a plot being hatched against the British Government by French and Russian spies. But the physical and mental strain of Kim's journey and secret work triggers a kind of breakdown, which makes him

doubt his place in the world. Can Kim find within himself the spiritual harmony which will restore his health and perhaps enable him to help the lama complete his great Search?

EXOTIC ADVENTURE

An exotic adventure story, *Kim* has more in common with American than European fiction of the time. Kipling particularly admired Mark Twain and, like Twain's *Huckleberry Finn, Kim* concerns a rebellious boyhood, and celebrates male friendship in a world where women are at best a distraction and at worst an active

---

| In the Background |

BUDDHISM

Kim's Tibetan lama is a follower of Gautama Buddha (right), the spiritual leader who began his teaching in the 6th century BC at Benares, the holy city. Buddha believed that all life is suffering, and that this is caused by desire or craving. He taught his disciples to follow the 'Middle Way' – between self-indulgence and self-mortification. This Middle Way leads to tranquillity, enlightenment and 'Nirvana'.

Like Hindus, Buddhists believe in reincarnation. The "Wheel of Life", which the lama draws, shows the cycle of life, death and rebirth which the lama wishes to leave. On illustrations of the Wheel of Life, the wheel is held by a monster, symbolizing the craving for life which traps people in the cycle of reincarnation.

"There would be a price upon his head in good time, as Lurgan Sahib had assured him; and if he talked foolishly now, not only would that price never be set, but Colonel Creighton would cast him off – and he would be left to the wrath of Lurgan Sahib and Mahbub Ali – for the short space of life that would remain to him."

nuisance. The journey of the lama and Kim down the Grand Trunk Road is rather like that of Huck and Jim along the Mississippi: indeed, the Road is referred to as "a river of life as nowhere else exists in the world".

Kim is, as Kipling wrote, a 'nakedly picaresque' novel – it takes the form of an adventure-filled journey. Yet the structure is held together by three themes that run throughout the book: the relationship between the lama and Kim; Kim's search for his own identity; and the role of the British in India. Eventually these three motifs merge into a single theme: who is Kim?

The contrast between Kim and the lama is a significant one. It is not only a contrast between youth and age, but also between curiosity and contemplation: a search for the meaning of life – or one's proper role in it – either through spiritual quietude (as in the case of the lama) or active service (as in Kim). For those who find the novel puzzling, the ambiguity resides in the question of who learns most from whom. The lama cautions Kim against the sin of pride and gives him an insight into the life of the spirit. Kim helps the lama to survive and teaches him the ways of the world.

SEARCH FOR IDENTITY

Kim's quest for identity takes him to the point of nervous exhaustion. Even at the outset, he is a mass of contradictions: an adolescent Irish Catholic who looks like an Indian and thinks in Hindustani. Through the novel he has to go through a bewildering array of disguises, at times looking like a European, at other times a Mohammedan. In addition, his spying activities compound the confusion since, by their very nature, they involve pretence, deception and acting. Where lies the core of such a character? Where does this "Little Friend of all the World" belong?

Part of the answer lies in Kim's identity as the son of an Irish soldier in an India under British rule, and in his ultimate adoption in the Great Game of British espionage. Some critics have suggested that, when Kim becomes a spy, he is betraying the Indian people, with whom he has spent his early life, and collaborating with their oppressors. But this is reading the novel with post-colonial hindsight. Kipling never saw the situation in those terms and, as George Orwell put it, always saw Imperialism as a 'sort of forcible evangelising'.

Through the lama, Kim gains a vision of the mystic heart of India. Through Colonel Creighton, he becomes an important instrument of what Kipling considered to be the benevolent British rule that preserved India from the throes of anarchy.

Kipling's unquestioning acceptance of British Imperialism is a major obstacle for some readers of his work. In contrast to the liberal critique of Forster's *A Passage to India, Kim* takes for granted the rightness of the political status quo in India. But Kipling is concerned above all to summon up the country in all its mystery and to follow the process by which a young boy can eventually come to terms with the complexities of his own character. That he achieved his aim brilliantly is beyond dispute.

Whispered threats
(below) While Kim is falling asleep beneath the stars he hears a plot to kill Mahbub Ali. Can he save his friend from death?

CHARACTERS IN FOCUS

Kim is teeming with a colourful cast of Eastern and British characters. The main focus is on the development of the two central characters, while the minor figures are there to serve the novel's purposes. The old soldier, for example, reveals the British partiality in the novel's rendering of colonial history. Kipling uses a reporter's ears and eyes: he conveys character through colloquial dialogue and vivid detail.

WHO'S WHO

Kim O'Hara The orphaned son of an Irish soldier in India. "A poor white of the very poorest", and the lama's *chela* (disciple).

Teshoo Lama A holy man from Tibet, who is searching for the sacred River that will free him from the Wheel of Life.

Mahbub Ali An Afghan horse-trader, who is in league with the British Secret Service.

Colonel Creighton An ethnologist (anthropologist), soldier and scholar, head of the Indian Survey Department (a cover for the British Secret Service in India).

Mr Bennett Protestant Chaplain of Kim's father's old regiment.

Father Victor Catholic priest of Kim's father's old regiment.

Lurgan Sahib Antique dealer of Simla: a magician who schools Kim in various memory games and disguises to prepare him for espionage work.

Hurree Chunder Mookerjee A fat erudite Bengali anthropologist who is a member of the Secret Service.

Curator of Lahore Museum An Englishman whose gifts to the lama are symbolic of the benevolence of the British in India; a partial portrait of Kipling's own father.

The Kulu woman An old harridan whom Kim and the lama meet on the Grand Trunk Road. She wants the lama to be 'her' priest.

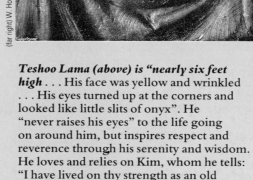

(far right) W. Holman Hunt: The lantern maker's courtship (detail). Birmingham City Art Gallery/Bridgeman Art Library

Teshoo Lama (above) is "nearly six feet high . . . His face was yellow and wrinkled . . . His eyes turned up at the corners and looked like little slits of onyx". He "never raises his eyes" to the life going on around him, but inspires respect and reverence through his serenity and wisdom. He loves and relies on Kim, whom he tells: "I have lived on thy strength as an old tree lives on the lime of a new wall."

Mary Evans Picture Library

"Bennett, the Church of England Chaplain of the regiment" (left), appears only briefly, but – significantly – he is one of the most unpleasant characters in the novel. When he first encounters the lama, "he looked at him with the triple-ringed uninterest of the creed that lumps nine-tenths of the world under the title of 'heathen'." He regards the lama's spiritual ideas as "gross blasphemy", and even goes to commit the unforgivable blunder of offering the holy man money in exchange for Kim. The character of Bennett illustrates the fact that Kipling was not entirely uncritical of the British in India. Bennett's unsympathetic nature stands in sharp contrast to other figures in the novel, and so highlights their particular qualities: the Catholic Father Victor's greater religious compassion; the lama's superior spirituality; and Creighton's more sensitive authoritarianism.

"Thoughtful, wise and courteous, but something of a small imp", Kim (left) is the endearing hero of the novel. Street-wise, skilful at using disguise and with a persuasive tongue, he cunningly manipulates others to the benefit of the lama and himself. His abilities, and his thirst for excitement and "newness", make him perfect material for the Secret Service. His nickname of "Little Friend of all the World" is double-edged: he gets on with all creeds, but his own identity is uncertain. "Who is Kim?" is one of the novel's themes.

Mahbub Ali, "the big burly Afghan (below) his beard dyed scarlet with lime", is a wealthy horse-trader, who is also involved in espionage (as C251B) for Colonel Creighton. He is portrayed by Kipling as a wily Pathan (of an Afghan tribe), happy under British rule – a characterization which many critics have seen as quite atypical of the time.

"A hulking, obese Babu whose stockinged feet shook with fat", Hurree Chunder Mookerjee (left) sounds unprepossessing, but is one of the most delightful characters in the novel. A Bengali with an MA from Calcutta University, he is always incongruously quoting Shakespeare. He comes into his own as 'R17' when he leads away Russian spies to give Kim a chance to escape with their papers. This act of courage is seen as significant for two reasons: because Bengalis are traditionally seen as being fearful, and because it shows how "great and desirable" is the cause of imperialism if it can "brazen the heart of a Bengali".

The tall "Englishman, dressed in black and white" to whom Kim delivers a message from Mahbub Ali is Colonel Creighton (below). He runs the Indian Survey Department, which doubles as the British Secret Service. Organizer of the "Great Game" of espionage, he is a freemason, a scholar and a soldier. He symbolizes Kipling's ideal of British rule in India: discreet, disciplined, compassionate but firm, and with an understanding of the country that enables him to exercise power with propriety and precision.

Richard Hook

Kipling Society

Reproduced by permission of Punch

PLAIN TALES

Kipling is one of the few authors to achieve distinction and popularity as a poet as well as a prose writer. But his greatest originality was as a writer of varied and spirited short stories.

In an age when most British writers of serious fiction were novelists who might occasionally publish short stories, Rudyard Kipling burst on to the literary scene with *Plain Tales from the Hills* (1888), *Wee Willie Winkie* (1888), *Soldiers Three* (1888), and *Life's Handicap* (1891). These and many subsequent collections of tales had a vividness and completeness that delighted readers and made Kipling a famous author.

Despite the fact that his masterpiece *Kim* is a novel, Kipling was primarily a short-story writer – arguably the greatest in the language. And, more than any other author, it was he who convinced British readers that the short story could be a separate art form, distinct from the novel and serving different literary purposes. Though celebrated for 'soldier tales, Indian tales, and tales of the fair sex', Kipling manipulated the short-story form with supreme virtuosity, whether he was dealing with occult events, school pranks, moments in history or animal fables.

INTUITION AND INSPIRATION

Underestimating his own strengths, Kipling 'dreamed for many years of building a veritable three-decker' novel, though he wisely never attempted it. He himself wrote that *The Light that Failed* (1890) was 'only a *conte* [story] – not a built book', and that *Kim* (1901) consisted of a series of episodes, 'nakedly picaresque and plotless', though of course none the worse for that. When he considered writing novels, his mother told him, 'You *know* you couldn't make a plot to save your soul'; and this was true in the sense that the complicated narrative developments and interactions found in most novels were alien to Kipling's temperament as an author.

In writing prose he relied on intuition to an uncommon extent, frequently insisting that 'the pen took charge' and that what he had written was 'honestly beyond my control'. Rather than inspiration, Kipling labelled this seemingly outside force his 'Daemon'. In his last book, the autobiographical *Something of Myself*, he advises, 'When your Daemon is in charge, do not try to think consciously. Drift, wait and obey.' He observed that,

though not unfailingly present, 'My Daemon was with me in the *Jungle Books, Kim,* and both Puck books, and good care I took to walk delicately, lest he should withdraw.'

His mastery lay in displaying the moment of truth or the all-illuminating episode – an art that gains in effectiveness with condensation. To this end, Kipling made a practice of laying aside each piece of work for long periods, picking it up from time to time in order to eliminate superfluities. He believed that 'a tale from which pieces have been raked out is like a fire that has been poked. One does not know the operation has been performed, but everyone feels the effects.'

This kind of craftsmanship and concentrated intensity is more generally found in

Kipling convalescing
(right) This portrait of Kipling was painted by his cousin Philip Burne-Jones when Kipling was recovering from serious illness in 1899. In spite of fairly frequent ill health, Kipling kept up an astonishing literary output. Even when too weak to write, he was thinking up ideas for new stories and articles.

A prolific journalist
Kipling's journalistic training and his experience of having to meet tight newspaper deadlines helped him to write with great speed and fluency. Below are two of the Indian newspapers on which he worked; and at the right he is shown as a journalist during the Boer War.

British Library

Weidenfeld Archive

poetry – Kipling's other vocation. Poetry's discipline gave him the extreme sensitivity to verbal music that characterizes his stories: 'There is no line of my verse or prose which has not been mouthed till the tongue has made all smooth, and memory, after many recitals, has mechanically stripped the grosser superfluities.'

APOSTLE OF IMPERIALISM

Fragments and complete poems are found scattered freely through the pages of his prose works, reflecting or commenting on the situations described in them. As a poet he was something of an odd-man-out among the aesthetes and decadents of the 1890s, writing of common men in a language that many critics found all too common – the cockney soldiers' talk of *Barrack-Room Ballads* (1892). Nor did his later verse, much of it concerned with great public issues, chime in comfortably with the 'modernism' of 20th-century poetry, despite Kipling's impeccable command of technique.

Both his convictions and the sources on which he drew (hymns, ballads, the

"the road to Mandalay, where the flying fishes play". *Recessional*, warning against imperial arrogance, achieved the status of a hymn, and *If* is one of the most-anthologized of all poems.

Kipling's reputation has fluctuated over the years. After the initial enthusiasm of the 1890s a reaction set in, especially among those who questioned the value of Britain's imperialist role. Kipling celebrated with ardour "the white man's burden" and Britain's "dominion over palm and pine" and became identified as the great apostle of imperialism. This was not in itself unusual or unacceptable; but in Kipling's case imperialism was accompanied by undeniably racist views and often hysterically reactionary political pronouncements. These alienated even mildly liberal or progressive readers.

CHILDREN'S STORIES

Only with the passage of time has it become possible to acknowledge and admire Kipling's genius without attempting to excuse his faults. In his best work, the artist in Kipling triumphed over the dogmatist, and he wrote with sympathy

music-hall) served to isolate him from his contemporary poets. They also helped him seize hold of the popular imagination. Few poets are quoted more frequently in ordinary speech, though many of Kipling's quotations, such as "East is East and West is West, and never the twain shall meet", are contentious in their racist sentiments. And singers still salute

Popular success
Kipling's work reached a vast audience. Books like Soldiers Three *were best-sellers and ballads like* Mandalay *were music-hall hits.*

and understanding of his fellow-beings – never more so than in *Kim*, where Indian characters are portrayed in all their variety, and a Tibetan lama is the most deeply

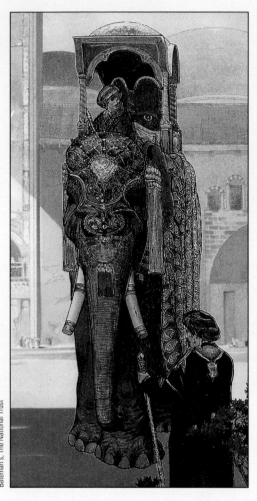

Illustrated classics
The humour and colour of Kipling's work made it marvellous material for illustrators. At right is Kipling's own illustration to Just So Stories, *of the Elephant's Child saying, '"Led go! You are hurting be!"' Left is a sumptuous scene from* Kim *from a 1908 edition of the book.*

appealing figure (next to Kim) in the book.

Many of Kipling's most enduring stories were written for an audience with no political leanings – children, whom he loved and understood. The *Jungle Books* (1894-95), and the *Just So Stories* (1902), with their elaborately incantatory style, have retained their classic status through all fashions and climates of opinion.

EVERYDAY HEROES

Kipling had an enormous influence on both life and literature. His work glamorized the East and the Empire, which he portrayed as heavy respon-sibilities shouldered for the benefit of the native peoples. In his idealized view, the Englishman was no mere exploiter, but served 'the Law' – an unwritten code that had to be lived up to at all costs. Unlike almost all previous writers, Kipling made the performance of everyday work one of his central concerns, taking as his heroes the subalterns, engineers and adminis-trators who kept civilization going, and delightedly manipulating their jargon as if it were a strange new poetic tongue. In these and many other ways Kipling enlarged and revitalized the literature of his time.

Master storyteller
*Kipling loved children and he loved telling them stories. One of his young cousins, Angela Mackail, later recalled how he could hold an infant audience spellbound: '*The Just So Stories *are a poor thing in print compared with the fun of hearing them told in Cousin Ruddy's deep unhesitating voice . . . There was an inimitable cadence, an emphasis of certain words, an exaggeration of certain phrases, a kind of intoning here and there which made his telling unforgettable.'*

Kipling was launched early in his career as an author, establishing himself as a poet and short-story writer when he was still in his early 20s, with *Departmental Ditties* (1886) and *Plain Tales from the Hills* (1888). British India provided the background for much of his work, and Britain's imperial role inspired his poetry in both the cockney rhymes of *Barrack-Room Ballads* (1892) and later, more solemn verses.

More personal concerns figure in Kipling's novel *The Light That Failed* (1890); this, like the boy's book *Stalky & Co.* (1899), is strongly autobiographical. Kipling had a particularly keen intuitative understanding of children, and in their various ways *The Jungle Books* (1894-95), *Just So Stories* (1902) and *Puck of Pook's Hill* (1906) forged enduring myths whose enchantment remains as potent as ever.

As the critic John Gross wrote, 'Kipling remains a haunting, unsettling presence, with whom we still have to come to terms.'

PLAIN TALES FROM THE HILLS

◆ 1888 ◆

Inspired by the places and people of India (right), Kipling's first book of fiction contains 40 stories, most of them written to a set length for the Lahore *Civil and Military Gazette*. Necessarily brief, these anecdotes and sketches create a colourful tapestry of Anglo-Indian life, ranging from the polo field to the barracks that house Learoyd, Mulvaney and Ortheris, the celebrated 'Soldiers Three' of later story collections. Other stories vary greatly in subject and mood. *The Gate of the Hundred Sorrows,* written when Kipling was only 18, gives a vivid word-picture of an opium-den, while in *Thrown Away* an over-sensitive subaltern kills himself after a dressing-down by his colonel and the affair has to be hushed up. A voice seemingly from the past robs a jockey of his victory and more in *The Broken-Link Handicap*, and in *Beyond the Pale* a Hindu girl is horribly punished for her affair with an Englishman.

Marianne North: The Himalayan foothills. Royal Botanic Gardens, Kew

THE LIGHT THAT FAILED

◆ 1890 ◆

A frustrated love affair (left) features in Kipling's first novel. The book is something of a puzzle, since the original magazine and American book version ended happily, whereas, when published in Britain, *The Light that Failed* was longer and unmistakably a tragedy; one explanation is that Kipling was writing of feelings he knew himself, for before he met his wife Carrie he had an attachment to a girl called Florence Garrard but found that his feelings for her were stronger than hers for him. Brought up together, Dick and Maisie come to love each other. But in his teens Dick is sent to the East, where he emerges as a successful war artist in Egypt and the Sudan. After a period of poverty and loneliness in London, he becomes famous and affluent. He encounters Maisie, now an art student, and his love is rekindled; but despite her lack of talent she is intent only on winning recognition. Then he gradually goes blind, and the masterpiece he rushes to complete is destroyed. Maisie seals his fate.

Fine Art Photographic Library. Inset Kipling Society

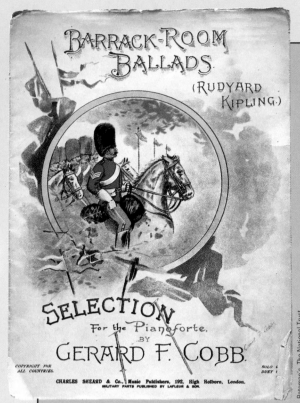

BARRACK-ROOM BALLADS AND OTHER VERSES

✦ 1892 ✦

Converted into popular songs (left), Kipling's army ballads attained widespread success. With their rendering of cockney speech and their thumping rhythms, they were unlike any British verse that had appeared before. Their subject too was original – the life of the common soldier, 'Tommy Atkins'. Kipling refused to ennoble or sentimentalize the British soldier, while insisting that in the last resort all civilization rested on his broad back ("For it's Tommy this, an' Tommy that, an' 'Chuck him out, the brute.'/But it's 'Saviour of 'is country'/when the guns begin to shoot"). One famous piece, *Danny Deever*, a chilling description of a military execution, is often considered to be Kipling's finest poem; the most famous is *Mandalay*, "somewheres east of Suez, where the best is like the worst,/Where there aren't no Ten Commandments an' a man can raise a thirst".

THE JUNGLE BOOKS

✦ 1894, 1895 ✦

Mowgli the Indian boy and Bagheera the panther (left) are two of the famous characters in the two *Jungle Books*, probably Kipling's greatest feats of purely imaginative storytelling. Baby Mowgli is saved from the tiger Shere Khan by wolves who bring him up as their own 'man-cub'. His other companions are Bagheera and Baloo the bear, who teaches him the law of the jungle. Capitalizing on his advantages as a human being, Mowgli is able to save the life of Akela, the ageing pack-leader of the wolves, and finally settles accounts with Shere Khan. But Mowgli's attempt to live among people is a failure, and when the villagers persecute his foster-parents, he takes a terrible revenge.

JUST SO STORIES
◆ 1902 ◆

Kipling's own illustration (right) conveys the magical quality of the fables in this much-loved book. Here we learn 'How the Whale got his Throat' and 'How the Camel got his Hump' (he said 'Humph!' once too often). *The Elephant's Child* tells how a young elephant travels to the 'banks of the great grey-green, greasy Limpopo River' to find out what the crocodile has for dinner – with unexpected results. In perhaps the best-known of all the stories, the Woman tames the dog, horse and cow. But one creature still declares 'I am the Cat who walks by himself.'

PUCK OF POOK'S HILL
◆ 1906 ◆

Visions from the past (below) animate this unusual historical fantasy. The scene is set at Pook's Hill near Kipling's house, Bateman's, in Sussex. Dan and Una, brother and sister, are enacting scenes from Shakespeare's *A Midsummer Night's Dream* before an audience of cows. While Dan is playing the part of the lively sprite

Puck, the real Puck appears and introduces himself. Then he uses his magic to call up a series of characters from early English history, and the book becomes a collection of linked stories. Their theme is the way in which all the people who have invaded the island – Romans, Saxons, Danes, Normans – have been absorbed into essential Englishness. The famous historian G. M. Trevelyan wrote of the 'marvellous historical sense' that Kipling displayed in such episodes as describe the Roman legionaries on Hadrian's Wall.

STALKY & CO
◆ 1899 ◆

Stalky, M'Turk and Beetle (above), the three heroes of this school story, are fictional counterparts of a real threesome at Kipling's school Westward Ho! – with the inkstained Beetle representing the boy Kipling. In a series of light-hearted episodes the fertile Stalky thinks up various pranks, of which masters who fail to 'play the game' are the chief victims. However, in one episode, 'The Moral Reformers', the three are asked by the school chaplain to investigate a suspected case of systematic bullying and, with his tacit approval, pay out the culprits in kind.

In the final episode, Stalky, now a man serving in the Indian Army, faces an attack by two hostile tribes and saves himself and his men by resorting to some tricky tactics quite worthy of his early schoolday exploits.

A SOLDIER'S LIFE

Kipling was the first writer to take the life of a common soldier as his subject. In India and South Africa he saw at first hand how hard and dangerous this life could be.

Kipling never served in the armed forces and he was halfway through his life before he witnessed warfare from the firing line. But his portrayal of the soldier's life in poetry and prose created the popular image of the British Army in late Victorian and Edwardian times. Indeed, many people at the time thought that he influenced not just their public image but the way soldiers saw themselves. Sir George Younghusband, for example, wrote in his book, *A Soldier's Memories in Peace and War* (1917):

'I myself had served for many years with soldiers, but never heard the words or expressions that Rudyard Kipling's soldiers used. Many a time did I ask my brother Officers whether they had heard them. No, never. But sure enough, a few years after, the soldiers thought, and talked, and expressed themselves exactly like Rudyard Kipling had taught them in his stories . . . Rudyard Kipling made the modern soldier.'

Younghusband's comments emphasize that it was essentially the world of the common soldier that Kipling explored. This was a new departure in English literature, for although the rank and file had figured often enough in earlier works (such as Shakespeare's *Henry V*), it had always been in a minor, supporting role. Kipling wrote as much about the barrack-room as the officers' mess.

SWEEPING REFORMS

Great changes were occurring in the British Army in the period when Kipling was growing up, and they were mainly the work of one remarkable man: Edward Cardwell (later Viscount Cardwell), Secretary of State for War from 1868 to 1874. When he took over at the War Office, the Army was notorious for including in its ranks the dregs of the population. (In 1831 the Duke of Wellington had described it as 'composed of the scum of the earth'.) Cardwell wanted a better quality of recruit. He wanted a more efficient army which could match the highly trained Continental forces. (In 1870-71, the Germans crushed France in the Franco-Prussian War with a show of awesome military power.)

One of Cardwell's first reforms was to abolish flogging in peace-time, a move strenuously opposed by most senior officers who regarded it as essential to discipline. By 1881, however, it was also abolished for soldiers on active service. In 1870 Cardwell also succeeded in reducing the minimum length of service from 12 years to six with a regiment and six 'on the reserve' (discharged but still available for conscription in wartime).

Cardwell's measures stimulated enlistment so successfully that in 1870 he was able to abolish 'bounty money' (a payment made for signing up). But soldiering continued to be a disreputable

C. J. Cramer-Roberts: Jamrud Fort, the Khyber Pass. India Office Library

Into battle
(below) The Boer War was the largest conflict the British Army had engaged in since the Napoleonic Wars.

Weidenfeld Archive

'A gentleman in kharki'
(above) This illustration to Kipling's poem 'The Absent-Minded Beggar' (1889) epitomizes his image of the staunch British private soldier or 'Tommy'.

George Scott: Royal Horse Artillery. National Army Museum

Cultures in conflict
(left) The British in India regarded themselves as the master race, and soldiers were discouraged from fraternizing with the Indians. Thus a soldier could spend a decade in the country and return home almost completely ignorant of its people and cultures.

Pillars of the Empire
(right) In this 1908 cartoon, Kipling is shown alongside Lord Kitchener, the most famous British soldier of his era. Part of the accompanying verse reads: 'When the Empire wants a stitch in her/Send for Kipling and for Kitchener.'

profession. When the future Sir William Robertson gave up a footman's job to join the Army in 1877, his mother told him she 'would rather see him dead than in a red coat'.

Robertson achieved the unprecedented feat of rising from the lowest rank in the army (private) to the highest (field marshal). But although Cardwell had put a stop to the practice of buying commissions and promotions, officers continued to be drawn mainly from the ranks of the aristocracy and gentry. The military establishment was extremely conservative and believed that a system

Family inspiration
(below) Kipling's sculptor father illustrated many of his son's works. This is his portrayal of Mulvaney from Soldiers Three.

Dedicated reformer
(above) Secretary of State
for War Edward Cardwell
did magnificent work in
improving army
conditions. He retired
exhausted in 1874.

Commander-in-chief
(above) Lord Roberts
was the most distinguished
soldier in India during
Kipling's time. On
occasion he consulted
Kipling about soldiers'
living conditions.

North-West Frontier
India is associated with
baking heat, but in the
Himalayan north things
were far different (photo-
graph taken during the
Second Afghan War).

good enough for the Dukes of Marlborough
and Wellington should be good enough for any-
one else.

Cardwell's reforms also included an important
improvement in equipment, with the adoption of
the Martini-Henry rifle, the Army's first proper
breech-loader, in place of less efficient muzzle-
loaders. The result of all these reforms was that the
Army, although still lagging behind the military
might of Germany and Russia, became a more
efficient and up-to-date organization. This was
clearly demonstrated in 1882, when the revolt of
Arabi Pasha in Egypt was firmly quashed – a far
cry from the bungling of the Crimean War.

'BLOOMIN' GOOD PAY'

The basic pay for a private in 1837, when Queen
Victoria came to the throne, was indeed the 'Shil-
lin' a day' of which Kipling wrote. By 1890 this
had risen to 1s 2d. However, stoppages were made
for food, cleaning equipment and other essentials,
so that a soldier pocketed much less. The official
attitude was that it was pointless paying the men
any more, as they would only spend it on drink.
Many civilians were worse off, and hunger could
be the best recruiting sergeant of all.

Everyday living conditions in garrison towns
were improving, with better cooking and bathing
facilities (though uninspired food). But a continuing source of misery for the rank and file was
the difficulty of leading a satisfactory married life.
A soldier had to obtain his commanding officer's
permission to marry, but the officer was severely
limited in the number of women he was allowed
to have living in barracks. If permission was
granted, the wife was designated as being 'on the
strength'. She moved wherever duty took her husband, or if she had to be left behind was granted a
small allowance. A wife married 'off the strength'
often faced great hardship, as she would be left to
fend for herself (and any children she might have)

if her husband happened to be posted elsewhere.

Although one of Cardwell's policies had been to
withdraw British troops from the self-governing
colonies, the Empire was still so large and far-
flung that a soldier was likely to spend much of his
term of duty thousands of miles away from home.
After the end of the Napoleonic Wars in 1815,
Europe enjoyed an unusually peaceful period, but
a constant military presence was maintained in
overseas territories, where there were frequent
skirmishes with rebellious subject peoples. In 1897,
the year of Queen Victoria's Diamond Jubilee, the
Daily Mail called the Victorian era 'emphatically
the period of small wars'.

India was by far the biggest drain on man-
power. Its territories were then even more vast
than they are today, incorporating Pakistan,
Bangladesh and part of present-day Burma. The
Indian Mutiny of 1857-58, when native troops
revolted against British rule, had shaken colonial
complacency, and although the Indian Army subsequently proved its loyalty, the British Army
kept a very careful watch on it. Generally, about a
third of the British Army was stationed in India.

DEADLY WEAPONS

When Kipling was in India as a journalist from
1882 to 1889, the subcontinent was enjoying a
period of calm after the end of the Second Afghan
War in 1880. For most soldiers, boredom and disease were deadlier enemies than the Afghans.

The most feared disease was cholera, for which
there was no known remedy. It struck with hor-
rifying suddenness – all might be well at morning
parade, but by nightfall a dozen men could be

Cushy living
(right) When fighting was
remote, life in India,
especially for officers,
could be 'cushy' – the
Hindi word for 'pleasant'.

suffering agonizing deaths, enduring acute diarrhoea, vomiting and crippling muscle cramps. It was generally believed that cholera was a kind of deadly, invisible cloud, and the only way to avoid it was to move the battalion or regiment to a temporary camp in a 'clean' area. This 'cholera-dodging' seldom worked. As Kipling wrote:

Since August when it started, it's been stickin' to our tail,

Though they've had us out by marches an' they've 'ad us back by rail;

But it runs as fast as troop trains, and we cannot get away,

An' the sick-list to the colonel makes ten more today.

PRIMITIVE SANITATION

The main cause of cholera was poor sanitation. The bacteria breed in places such as cesspits, and are transmitted by drinking fouled water or eating food contaminated by flies. Florence Nightingale's stress on good hygiene in the Crimea had not gone entirely unheeded, and some of the barracks built in India were airy and pleasant compared with their bleak, cramped equivalents in England. But by today's standards, sanitation was primitive and the stink of the latrines was present day and night. Kipling himself suffered the effects of Calcutta's bad sanitation and his years in India left him a legacy of ill health.

Given the discomfort and monotony of their lives, it is not surprising that soldiers' tempers frayed easily. The phrase 'hot weather shootings' has been used to describe the outbursts of violence that could erupt between comrades-in-arms. The horrible sequel – the military execution – formed

BBC Hulton Picture Library

Officers and men
The British Army endured primitive living conditions during the Boer War in South Africa (1899-1902). Above is an officers' mess, looking more like a workmen's hut. Right, a drummer boy (the minimum age was 14) writes home. The Army Post Office in South Africa handled 170,000 letters a week.

Waidenfeld Archive

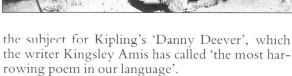

National Army Museum

the subject for Kipling's 'Danny Deever', which the writer Kingsley Amis has called 'the most harrowing poem in our language'.

Sunday was the day most hated by soldiers. The tedium and bullying of the drill square were replaced by Church Parade – which was generally agreed to be even worse and was deeply resented as it took up so much of a 'free' day. Such religious observance remained compulsory until after World War II, but crafty recruits (perhaps tipped off by old hands) could get round it by claiming to belong to some Nonconformist group such as the Plymouth Brethren.

Drinking and sex with prostitutes provided light relief for soldiers in India, as elsewhere. In 1868 commanding officers were empowered to fine soldiers for drunkenness, and in 1876 over a quarter of the whole army was fined. Venereal disease was a scourge, and it has been estimated that at any one time about five per cent of the Army would be unfit for duty because of it. Lord Roberts, commander-in-chief in India from 1885 to 1893, was a member of the Army Temperance Association and one of the many senior officers who frowned on drinking or debauchery.

Despite the great discomforts of life in India, many soldiers preferred to do their service there rather than in England. At times there was little

serious fighting, and if a soldier could come to terms with the climate he had a relatively easy life, for native servants did the worst menial tasks.

In his autobiography, *Something of Myself* (1937), Kipling tells us that he based the soldiers in his Indian stories on real-life characters he had met in Lahore. He obviously loved soldiers' company, but after he left India in 1889, it was not until the Boer War of 1899-1902 that he again came into close, regular contact with the Army. In January 1900 he sailed for Cape Town to combine work as a journalist with convalescence in the sunny climate. His first sight of serious fighting came on 29 March 1900 at the Battle of Karee Siding, an indecisive encounter but one he found thrilling.

WAR IN SOUTH AFRICA

The war against the Boers (descendants of Dutch colonists) was entirely different from any the British Army had experienced. The opponents were not brave but under-equipped native people; they were resourceful guerillas, superb horsemen and crack shots who could exploit the terrain. Winston Churchill wrote in 1899, 'The individual Boer, mounted, in a suitable country is worth four or five regular soldiers.' Against them the skills that looked impressive on the parade ground were useless, and the British suffered a series of humiliating defeats before their sheer weight of numbers turned the tide.

Kipling spent about eight months in South Africa during the war, working on an army newspaper and visiting the wounded. Like many others he was appalled by the conditions endured by the soldiers, among whom typhoid and dysentery were rife. The stench of a camp infected with dysentery could be smelled a mile away.

A fascinating insight into the life of an ordinary British soldier during the war is revealed in the diary kept by Private Frederick Tucker. On 12 March 1900 Tucker wrote: 'We were treated to soft bread again in lieu of biscuits; this was the first

100

A heroes' welcome
(above) The City Imperial Volunteers are received in splendour in the Guildhall after returning from the Boer War in 1900. Kipling helped to transform the image of the soldier from 'scum of the earth' to source of national pride.

For King and Country
Kipling's son was one of the countless young men to die in the Great War.

bread we had tasted since 12 February. We were not sorry for the change, for a month on biscuits of the army type is enough for any man – even if his teeth are like steel.'

In addition, the rain and cold of the winter nights caused much misery. On 28 May 1900 (winter in the southern hemisphere) Tucker wrote: 'It was too cold to sleep and in the morning I found that my top blanket was quite wet and stiff . . . I tried to make some coffee but found my water bottle full of ice.'

The handling of the war (particularly the use of concentration camps for Boer women and children) caused much anti-imperialist and anti-British feeling, but it was also during this war that the British public first really took the common soldier to their hearts. The number of soldiers sent to South Africa was huge – about 450,000 – and almost every town and village in the country contributed its share of men. Thus there was an unprecedented sense of personal involvement. This was heightened by the jingoistic popular Press and Kipling's patriotic verse.

WAR GRAVES COMMISSIONER

Kipling's South African poems include the famous 'Boots' – but generally the verse and stories inspired by the war do not rank high in his literary output. Perhaps close contact with the horrific aspects of warfare cooled some of his patriotic ardour. This process was completed in World War I – particularly after his son was killed in action – when his work reeked of despair.

Kipling kept his sense of duty and loyalty, however, and in 1917 he became one of the War Graves Commissioners. He worked for the Commission for the rest of his life, and it was he who suggested such words as those engraved at the entrance to each war cemetery: 'Their name liveth for evermore'. It is this dignified work that stands as the most fitting memorial to his special relationship with the British soldier.

BIBLIOGRAPHY

Ball, Stuart, *Baldwin and the Conservative Party*. Yale University Press (New Haven, 1988)

Bayly, C. A., *Indian Society and the Making of the British Empire*. Cambridge University Press (New York, 1988)

Bloom, Harold, ed., *Daniel Defoe*. Chelsea House (New York, 1987)

Boas, Louise S., *A Great Rich Man: The Romance of Sir Walter Scott* (reprint of 1929 edition). Richard West (Philadelphia, 1978)

Broehl, Wayne G., Jr., *Crisis of the Raj*. University Press of New England (Hanover, 1986)

Brown, Hilton, *Rudyard Kipling*. Haskell Booksellers (Brooklyn, 1974)

Burne-Jones, Edward, *The Pre-Raphaelite Drawings of Edward Burne-Jones*. Dover Publications (New York, 1981)

Carswell, D., *Life of Sir Walter Scott*. Haskell Booksellers (Brooklyn, 1971)

Chadwick, William, *Life and Times of Daniel Defoe* (reprint of 1859 edition). Burt Franklin (New York, 1969)

Chambers, Robert, *Traditions of Edinburgh*. Cambridge University Press (New York, 1987)

Clemens, Cyril, *A Chat with Rudyard Kipling*. Folcroft (Folcroft, 1943)

Davie, Donald, *A Gathered Church: The Literature of the English Dissenting Interest, 1700-1930*. Oxford University Press (New York, 1978)

Fellows, Otis E., and Torrey, Norman L., *The Age of Enlightenment*. Prentice Hall (Englewood Cliffs, 1971)

Finley, Gerald, *Turner and George IV in Edinburgh, 1822*. Columbia University Press (New York, 1982)

Gregg, Edward, *Queen Anne*. Routledge, Chapman & Hall (New York, 1984)

Greig, J. Y., *David Hume*. Garland Publishing (New York, 1983)

Hewitt, David, *Scott on Himself*. Longwood Publishing Group (Wolfeboro, 1981)

Hopkins, Robert T., *Rudyard Kipling: The Story of a Genius*. Folcroft (Folcroft, 1977)

Keen, Maurice, *Chivalry*. Yale University Press (New Haven, 1984)

Kent, Harold W., *Dr. Hyde and Mr. Stevenson*. Charles E. Tuttle (Rutland, 1973)

Ker, William, *Sir Walter Scott*. Haskell Booksellers (Brooklyn, 1974)

Lee, Emanuel, *To the Bitter End: A Photographic History of the Boer War, 1899-1902*. Viking Penguin (New York, 1986)

Maixner, Paul, *Robert Louis Stevenson: The Critical Heritage*. Routledge, Chapman & Hall (New York, 1981)

Mason, Shirlene, *Daniel Defoe and the Status of Women*. Eden Press (Cheektowaga, 1978)

McLaren, M., *Stevenson and Edinburgh*. Haskell Booksellers (Brooklyn, 1974)

McLynn, Frank, *Charles Edward Stuart: A Tragedy in Many Acts*. Routledge, Chapman & Hall (New York, 1988)

Mitchell, John O., *Burns and His Times*. Folcroft (Folcroft, 1973)

Moors, H. J., *With Stevenson in Samoa*. Richard West (Philadelphia, 1973)

Rao, K. Bhaskara, *Rudyard Kipling's India*. University of Oklahoma Press (Norman, 1967)

Richetti, John J., *Daniel Defoe*. G. K. Hall (Boston, 1987)

Ritchie, Robert C., *Captain Kidd and the War Against the Pirates*. Harvard University Press (Cambridge, 1986)

Roberts, Brian, *Cecil Rhodes: Flawed Colossus*. W. W. Norton (New York, 1988)

Saposnik, Irving S., *Robert Louis Stevenson*. G. K. Hall (Boston, 1974)

Shanks, Edward, *Rudyard Kipling: A Study in Literature and Political Ideas* (reprint of 1941 edition). Century Bookbindery (Philadelphia, 1985)

Steuart, J. A., *Robert Louis Stevenson: Man and Writer* (reprint of 1924 edition). Richard West (Philadelphia, 1973)

Thomson, George M., *Sir Francis Drake*. David & Charles (North Pomfret, 1988)

Warner, Philip, *Kitchener: The Man Behind the Legend*. Atheneum (New York, 1986)

Wigfield, W. MacDonald, *The Monmouth Rebels, 1685*. St. Martin's Press (New York, 1985)

Williamson, Kennedy, *W. E. Henley*. Haskell Booksellers (Brooklyn, 1974)

Wilt, Judith, *Secret Leaves: The Novels of Walter Scott*. University of Chicago Press (Chicago, 1986)

Zimmerman, Everett, *Defoe and the Novel*. University of California Press (Berkeley, 1974)

INDEX